BUILDERS OF HOPE

ALSO BY WANDA URBANSKA

The Heart of Simple Living: 7 Paths to a Better Life

Less Is More: Embracing Simplicity for a Healthy Planet, a Caring Economy and Lasting Happiness (with Cecile Andrews)

Nothing's Too Small to Make a Difference (with Frank Levering)

Christmas on Jane Street: A True Story (with Billy Romp)

Moving to a Small Town: A Guidebook for Moving from Urban to Rural America (with Frank Levering)

Simple Living: One Couple's Search for a Better Life (with Frank Levering)

Official Secrets

The Singular Generation: Young Americans in the 1980s

BUILDERS OF HOPE

A Social Entrepreneur's Solution for Rebuilding America

WANDA URBANSKA

Builders of Hope:
A Social Entrepreneur's Solution for Rebuilding America
By Wanda Urbanska
Foreword by Founder and CEO Nancy Welsh

Distributed by:
John F. Blair, Publisher
1406 Plaza Drive
Winston-Salem, NC 27103
www.blairpub.com

Manufactured in the United States of America
Printed on recycled paper originating from sustainable forests
Page design by The Roberts Group
Cover image by Jennifer Kromhout

Library of Congress Cataloging-in-Publication Data

Urbanska, Wanda, 1956-
Builders of Hope : a social entrepreneur's solution for rebuilding America / by Wanda Urbanska ; foreword by founder and CEO Nancy Welsh.
p. cm.
Includes index.
ISBN 978-0-89587-568-6 (alk. paper)
1. Welsh, Nancy, 1967- 2. Builders of Hope (Organization) 3. Housing rehabilitation–United States. 4. Housing development–Social aspects–United States. 5. Working poor–Housing–United States. 6. Community development–United States. 7. Social entrepreneurship–United States. I. Title.
HD7293.U67 2011
363.5'57630973–dc23

2011022420

CONTENTS

FOREWORD
BY NANCY WELSH

When I was a little girl, my mother used to read me a picture book called *The Little House.* Even at my tender age, the simple children's tale made an indelible impression.

It depicts the ominous turn of events for a charming bungalow in the country. In the story, as the years go by, this sweet, soulful home—built to last for generations—is confronted with urban sprawl. It finds itself in the midst of massive development—enveloped by wide roads, bustling traffic, and towering skyscrapers. The property where the little house sits is rezoned; the place is abandoned and boarded up and falls into a state of disrepair. Miraculously, the little house is discovered and purchased by an ancestor of the original owner, who rescues it and has it physically relocated to the "new" countryside. Completely rehabilitated, the little house is transformed into a dream home for an appreciative young family once again.

Looking back on it now, I see that this classic 1942 book by Virginia Lee Burton may well have planted the seeds for my own personal passion to rescue teardowns and turn them into beautiful, affordable, and safe housing for deserving families. Indeed, the mission of the nonprofit organization I founded in 2006, Builders of Hope, bears an uncanny parallel to the story line of *The Little House.*

The challenges that I faced—and continue to face on a daily basis—have been many, and I draw inspiration from tales of perseverance and overcoming great odds. As a woman breaking into the construction field with ideas not yet pursued by my male counterparts, I have come face to face with my share of brick walls. Discrimination, chauvinism, and exclusionary practices posed obstacles in starting the organization I believed in and have seen through early challenges to great success.

Pioneers in any field encounter barriers that can become opportunities if they allow them to be. Indeed, without the brick walls, I may not have been challenged to create new solutions, to think, as the cliché goes, outside the box. Proactive problem solving and strategic implementation were necessary in garnering respect from the "good ole boys" club in which I found myself. Innovation and entrepreneurial-style management not only propelled Builders of Hope past the barriers but fostered increasing acceptance of our model while moving America toward a new paradigm for the creation of affordable, sustainable housing.

If you have a passion to make a positive difference in the world, to do the right thing for the right reason, there are virtually no limits to what you can achieve. When you step out of the materialistic "what's in it for me?" mindset and become inspired to act in the interest of your community, you will be amazed at what you are capable of doing.

During media interviews and presentations around the country, I'm frequently asked for advice to help budding entrepreneurs find their way—something that's especially relevant in today's economy, in which innovation is the surest way to create jobs. My advice is to find your passion and identify opportunities that will allow you to make a difference in your local community. Start small, think small, and work through the details of practical implementation of your idea. Be sure to test and perfect any new model locally, ensuring a solid foundation before you give thought to replication.

When I'm asked where people can look for inspiration, I recommend starting in their own backyards by identifying unmet community needs. And I recommend searching for *solutions that provide systemic change*, rather than a quick fix. Today's successful social entrepreneur challenges herself to redefine the problem and then address the core need with fresh solutions. Work hard, know the clientele you wish to serve, then do the work first yourself that you will later ask others to do. If you can swing it, invest your own money in the idea before asking others to fund it for you. Pay for programs and services before you pay yourself. Be frugal with your funds and efficient with your time.

Your "return on investment" is the ability to positively and permanently impact your community. At the end of your life, it will not be the balance of your personal treasury that you will be remembered for, but the benefit to those lives and communities where you've had a lasting impact.

Ideas and inspirations that cultivate your passions and interests and tie you to real issues are quite often the making of personal transformation. A change-making evolution is one that quickens your soul and brings you most fully alive. The insights gained, coupled with the accumulation of experiences over a lifetime, uniquely qualify each of us to identify solutions that encourage others to change the way they think, change the way they work, and perhaps one day change the world. It is my deepest wish that Builders of Hope will inspire you on your path.

SPECIAL THANKS FROM NANCY WELSH

To begin with, I would like to thank my mom, Jackie Welsh, for all of her encouragement and support. Without her generosity and inspiration, none of Builders of Hope's success would have been possible. To my children—Ben, Jack, Anna, and Austin—I offer thanks for volunteering, working on job sites, setting up for and participating in special events, and cheering me on every step of the way. All four have been a part of Builders of Hope from the very beginning, and their support and encouragement have meant the world to me. A special thank-you goes to my brother David for believing enough in the mission to both provide financial support and join the staff. I thank all of my family for their patience and endurance in getting Builders of Hope launched and running and for their individual contributions to the success of the organization and the writing of this book.

My heartfelt thanks goes to John Jenkins for sharing the vision, for teaching me everything I know about construction, and for mastering more than he ever wanted to know about the amazing world of house moving and reconstruction! I thank Lew Schulman for jumping headlong into our start-up organization and creating standardized processes and procedures. Lew helped develop and manage our unique business model, making it replicable nationally. We wouldn't be where we are today without him.

I cannot express sufficient gratitude to the members of the board of directors, past and present, for their commitment, wise counsel, and enormous contributions of time and talent. Our founding members—Sandra Martin Clark, Carolyn Grant, and Peter Adams—played a significant role in our history. Sandy and Peter continue to serve, along with Victoria Phillips, Scott

Stone, Tim Goettel (whose hours of involvement and pro bono legal counsel I will never forget), and the Reverend Phil Brickle (our first homeowner in Barrington Village).

I thank Darryl Colwell and the entire construction staff. There would be no Builders of Hope without them; they are the legs on which we stand. Their innovation in sustainability, attention to quality, and ultimate affordability for those we serve are unparalleled in the industry. A special shout-out goes to Chris Lewis, Ben Britt, and Brandon Pearson for perfecting the model on the ground.

The fingerprints of every volunteer, work-mentee, and donor will always remain on our organization. For their passion and commitment, I am forever grateful. Each staff member has contributed a piece of who we are today. I would particularly like to thank Eric Hostettler, Stan Wilson, Dennis Boothe, Emily Egge, Lindsay Locke, Lisa Kaiser-Long, Joyce Kohn, Juliette Dolle, Shannon Bass, Blake Rothwell, Landon Lovelace, and Charlotte Rybinski. Among those pioneers in our satellite offices, my deep appreciation goes to Brenda Hayden, Rick Gesslinger, Chris Dodd, Zac Lytle, and Bennett Miller for their successful efforts in establishing and managing new Builders of Hope projects.

I thank Mayor Charles Meeker of Raleigh for following our work early on and for believing in us enough to partner in the development of a model sustainable, affordable housing community for the city. Most significantly, I want to thank the communities in which we work and the homeowners themselves for embracing the Builders of Hope model. The homeowners have become true pioneers in the revitalization of troubled communities by purchasing our rescued homes. They have also proven to be incredible advocates and ambassadors. I thank them for their belief in our model, their investment in our homes—now *their* homes—their commitment to sustainable building and living, and their willingness to move their families to communities in need of serious revitalization. Together, family, staff, community, and clients are responsible for who we are today.

Finally, I want to thank Wanda Urbanska, who, after writing an article about Builders of Hope for *Natural Home* magazine, understood a book was waiting to blossom. She is a wonderful collaborator and friend. The team at John F. Blair, Publisher—Carolyn Sakowski, Angela Harwood, Margaret Couch, and Steve Kirk—has been a pleasure to work with. I thank them for bringing *Builders of Hope* to life on the page and into the marketplace.

ACKNOWLEDGMENTS

I have never written a book in a greater number of locations or under more varying circumstances than this one. The idea germinated over coffee with Nancy Welsh at the Sunflower House in Mount Airy, North Carolina, in August 2009. I conducted my initial research in Raleigh and Durham before I departed in October 2009 on my sabbatical in Warsaw, Poland, where I began writing in earnest. In January 2010, Nancy traveled in the bitter cold to Warsaw, where we met in *kawiarnie* and at kitchen tables to move the work forward. I completed the manuscript in the offices of Builders of Hope in Raleigh in the fall of 2010.

First and foremost, I would like to thank Nancy Welsh for her partnership and collaboration and for her remarkable responsiveness in answering my barrage of questions and e-mails about the many facets of Builders of Hope while running her booming operation and tending to the demands of her large family. Other individuals who deserve specific mention include my office mates at Builders of Hope, Liza Martina, Dennis Boothe, Shannon Bass, Landon Lovelace, Darryl Colwell, Lew Schulman, Stan Wilson, Alex Henzel, and Lisa Kaiser-Long.

Inspirations for my work on this book and my interest in preservation and sustainable housing solutions include Linda Fuller and her husband, the late Millard Fuller, to whom this book is dedicated. Another inspiration is Mary Bishop, the extraordinary reporter for the *Roanoke Times & World News*, who wrote a remarkable series of articles on the destruction of an African-American community in inner-city Roanoke, which stayed in my mind for many years after its publication in the mid-1990s. Mary even mailed to me in Warsaw a copy of the original yellowing series, along with Mindy Fullilove's book—a copy autographed to Mary's husband, Dan. Talk about trust!

Thanks go to Robyn Griggs-Lawrence, former editor in chief of *Natural Home* magazine, who commissioned my original article on Builders of Hope that reeled me into the topic. I appreciate the support of Jessica Kellner of *Natural Home* and Bryan Welsh, head of Ogden Publications, along with K. C. Compton and others there.

I am obliged to many friends and family members, including my beloved sister, Jane Urbanski Robbins, my always supportive mother, Marie Urbanski Whittaker, and my son, Henry Urbanski Levering. Special thanks go to Aunt Ruth Kelley and Aunt Margaret Corbin-Raley. I am appreciative of Malgorzata Dzieduszycka-Ziemilska for housing Henry and me in Warsaw, Irene Tomaszewski, Ewa Wierzynska, Consul General Ewa Junczyk-Ziomecka of the Republic of Poland, my cousins Monika Malcher and Grzegorz Urbanski, and Allen and Betsy Paul, who have become as close as family. I would like to thank my dear friends Ann Vaughn, Ann Williams, Ann Belk, Bonni Brodnick, and Liz Brody for being there, always. I was also delighted to discover my "new family" in Raleigh—cousins Tom and Gail Blalock and their children and grandchildren.

Come and let's get it together.
Let's make it a showplace again. . . .
Help us make this a proud street again.
Help us make you a proud people again.

—Charles Joyner

CHAPTER 1

THE BUILDERS OF HOPE CREATION STORY

Nancy Welsh's experiences as an advertising executive, wife, mother, and community activist and leader—her passion for social justice and her willingness to make a substantial investment from family money to start Builders of Hope—bring an innovative organization to life. This profile in gutsy but grounded risk taking introduces Welsh's first partners, shows how she was inspired to enter the construction field and create the Builders of Hope model, and seeks to inspire other social entrepreneurs to take action.

Nancy Welsh's interest in construction was born from a two-story addition and remodel on her home in northwest Raleigh, North Carolina. The year was 2004, and Welsh and her husband had decided to convert their garage into a family room and to add a bonus room, office, full bath, and laundry area overhead to accommodate the needs of their growing family of four children, two dogs, and visiting relatives and friends. They built their new garage from scratch adjacent to where the old one had been.

Welsh's career had been in sales and advertising before she put it on hold to play the role of full-time wife and mother. On the casual recommendation of a neighbor down the street who had used a contractor named John Jenkins for a similar project, Welsh set up an appointment. It was a meeting that proved providential not only in her development and evolution but in sparking the creation of an organization that would come to be known as Builders of Hope.

At that first meeting, Welsh and Jenkins clicked, and she hired him on the spot. The two recognized each other as kindred spirits. Both were unorthodox and did not conform to the stereotypes of the positions they held in society. Welsh was a far cry from the glamorous, privileged housewife she resembled—from the kind of woman who picked out the colors, wrote the checks, and went off to play bridge. The real Nancy Welsh was a singular combination of brains, creativity, and drive and had a strong Christian faith at her core. For his part, Jenkins was no surly chauvinist contractor who would cringe at the thought of letting a client—especially a female—put her nose into his business. He was an articulate, well-educated, even courtly man who had come to construction in a rather roundabout way as a second career.

The First Teacher

A West Virginia native, John Jenkins started out in radio and television broadcasting, initially in Huntington, West Virginia, and later as general manager at a Christian radio station in Asheville, North Carolina. When he left broadcasting in 1989, he realized he wanted to return to his first love: construction. He had always enjoyed contributing to the built environment by working with his hands, at his own pace. His goal was never to make a fortune but only to provide a decent living for his family. In middle age, with his only real experience working construction crews during summers in college, he knew he would have to start at the bottom.

Jenkins shakes his head, conjuring up a comical memory of his first assignment: carrying lumber at a construction project in Durham. "When I showed up at the job site driving my BMW, all the workers looked at me like, 'What in the world is *he* doing here?'" Jenkins proved to be a keeper. He quickly demonstrated that he could work as hard as anyone else and wasn't above any part of the job. Before long, he branched out on his own, starting a one-man company that built decks and screened porches. This rapidly evolved into house remodels, additions, and some new-home construction.

In February 2004, when Jenkins began work on Nancy Welsh's house on Clark's Branch Drive in Raleigh, little did he imagine that he had taken on not only a job but a disciple—and ultimately a new course in life. Welsh was magnetically drawn to the process, right down to the most minute detail. She wanted to know how to tear out and build back, how materials were chosen, how rooms were framed, wired, and insulated, how sheetrock was hung. As she observed the giant dumpster filling in her front yard, she wondered where the waste materials were hauled and if any could be salvaged. She watched wide-eyed as an ever-changing cast of subcontract employees came and went, all with their specialties and compelling—and often heart-wrenching—life stories. Before long, to expedite the process and to save money, Welsh rolled up her sleeves and offered herself up as a volunteer laborer to the man she had hired.

Jenkins had never heard an offer quite like hers. He accepted immediately. If he harbored any initial doubts that she might slow the process, they were quickly retired. Jenkins found Welsh to be "easy to work with, a fast learner," and, quite simply, a pleasure to have around. "Nancy is a super-wonderful person," he says.

The respect and admiration flowed both ways. Welsh describes Jenkins as "patient and caring, a natural-born teacher." She not only enjoyed his company but relished seeing how everything fit together. Before long, she realized she had a knack for the work. She made friends with the circular saw, the electric sander, and the air-gun nailer. "I was surprised to find out how much fun it was to staple the shoe molding at the baseboard," she recalls.

"Going in, I thought my work on our house was going to be a one-time thing," Welsh says. But construction opened a whole new world to her and helped take her mind off her nonstop duties as the mother of her brood of young, challenging children, who at the time ranged from five to 12 years of age. At the end of a workday, Welsh was not only physically exhausted but had something tangible to show for her efforts.

When the remodel project was completed on September 3, 2004—just in time to celebrate her husband's 40th birthday and open the house to out-of-town guests—Welsh did not want to wash her hands of all the racket and mess. She realized she didn't want the work to stop. "The truth is," she says, "I got hooked."

Cross Link Road: Learning by Doing

Some people talk long and hard about their dreams, deferring them for a future that never materializes. Nancy Welsh was not one of them. A self-described "can-do, take-charge" kind of person, Welsh quickly hatched a plan to put her construction skills to the test. She invited Jenkins to work with her once again—this time on a for-profit venture she would finance with her inheritance.

In March 2005, Welsh identified a foreclosure property in southeast Raleigh—a house on Cross Link Road, just four minutes from the beltway surrounding the city's inner loop—that seemed to cry out for rehab. She jumped in and worked side by side with Jenkins, who mentored her in framing, wiring, sheetrocking, and deconstruction. The two did the majority of the labor themselves. Welsh went off to work every day wearing blue jeans from Goodwill and a pink leather tool belt.

John Jenkins, shown here at Barrington Village, was Nancy Welsh's first teacher and construction mentor.

The Cross Link Road house—a 1,200-square-foot, 1940s brick rancher—sat on a lot just under an acre in size. Welsh and Jenkins realized that with some creative thinking, they could fit two more homes onto that parcel. Once they subdivided the property, though, they saw that the first house was awkwardly positioned, straddling the lot lines. What to do?

Jenkins remembered seeing a television program in which a house was moved. Having no experience with the process, he was reluctant at first to try it. But with Welsh's encouragement, the two decided to give it a go. "We interviewed house movers and found one that was willing to give us a good break on pricing," she says.

That First House Move

On the appointed day, the first house was moved from its original position just 75 feet west to center it on Lot No. 1. Though the learning curve was steep for Jenkins and Welsh, and though they

Welsh and Jenkins's first long-distance house move and rehab on Cross Link Road

experienced a few dicey moments, the move went off without a hitch. It was magical in its way, seeing a house hoisted into the air from its foundation in one piece and moved to its new place in the world. The process transfixed Welsh and planted an important seed in her brain. If that old house could be moved so easily, she wondered, weren't hundreds of other adequate but dated houses all over the city—and maybe thousands all over America—just calling out for rescue and rehab?

Once the house was moved, the partners went to work transforming it into what they hoped would be a salable property. Solidly constructed, with great bones, the house had an excellent layout and beautiful hardwood floors. Welsh speculated that a previous owner had started a remodel with the installation of new windows but had run out of money before completing the job. Jenkins and Welsh gutted the house by tearing out the sheetrock and insulation, removing the wiring and plumbing, and basically stripping it to its shell.

The only significant design change they made was taking down a kitchen wall that abutted a small corner den, thus opening up the interior while creating an eat-in kitchen. While they were at it, they carved out space in the kitchen for a stackable washer and dryer. Prior to the house move, they had removed the brick fireplace, which opened up space for a built-in desk. Casting around for ways to reuse materials that might otherwise go to waste, Welsh spotted an old, undamaged door that could be repurposed as a desktop for that space. As they put the finishing touches on the house—including painting the trim a cheerful yellow and installing an old-fashioned front-porch swing—Welsh found the process as rewarding in its own way as remodeling her own home.

Going the Prefab Route

For Lot No. 2, Welsh and Jenkins briefly entertained but quickly dismissed the idea of putting up a stick-built home. They realized they couldn't compete in price with track builders in the area, who would beat them with their economies of scale. Prefabricated modular housing intrigued Welsh, who had heard that factory-built homes represented the future of new construction. She did some research and settled on a first-rate builder, Hand Crafted Homes of Henderson, North Carolina. She selected a 1,500-square-foot Craftsman-style house with three bedrooms and two baths. Though the home was well engineered and of high quality, the modular process turned out to be more expensive than the initial estimates suggested. Unplanned expenses—such as those involved with seaming work and the hiring of modular cranes to put the house together—added significantly to the bottom line.

House No. 3: Back to Rehab

Maybe the stars aligned in some inexplicable way to send Welsh back to where she had started with the development. Or maybe it was the fact that the house mover wore her down by calling every week, pestering her about all the terrific teardown houses with which he could provide her. Whatever the case, when the house mover offered up an adorable early-1960s rancher slated for demolition, Welsh bit the bullet. The house—which belonged to an IBM employee who was building his dream (read: much larger) house on the same lot—would have to be moved 18 miles to the Cross Link property. This time, the move proved surprisingly easy despite the much longer distance.

Once House No. 3 was anchored on its new foundation, only a modicum of work was required to bring it up to market standards. The main rehab and renovation jobs were adding a second bath, opening up the kitchen, and building a deck with French doors to adjoin the dining area. The biggest design challenge was making room for the second bath. "We squeezed out some space between two bedrooms to create a Jack and Jill bathroom, making it accessible to both rooms," Welsh says. "It was an absolute dollhouse when we were finished. I can't imagine anyone not being thrilled to live there."

Welsh bought a Bobcat with a clamshell bucket to help move dirt so she could work on the landscaping disturbed by the remodel. Jenkins trained her to use it. Running the Bobcat became her favorite job, much to the surprise of the many male subcontractors, who would take a minute to watch. Welsh's excitement over her personal bulldozer quickly spread to her kids. "All of a sudden, Mom became cool," she says, recalling how her youngest child, Austin, and his friends clamored for rides on the Bobcat at his fifth birthday party.

Lessons Learned

Developing the trio of homes on the Cross Link Road property offered Welsh a hands-on learning laboratory in the affordable housing world. Even as she worked on the homes, Welsh's mind was racing ahead to the next phase. Each of the three houses presented a distinct model that she would consider as she began sketching plans for future development. What's more, seeing how much impact her modest investment had on one neighborhood, she started to imagine what might happen if she were to create an entire affordable housing community from scratch.

Welsh's first idea was to use modular units for the new development she was sketching out in her mind, but the cost overruns on the Cross Link Road prefab house gave her pause. Not only were the costs higher than she had projected, but she quickly realized that public perception at the time—which equated prefabricated housing with the flimsy mobile homes of the past—had not caught up with the reality of state-of-the-art modular construction. As it turned out, the two rehabbed houses that book-ended the modular unit provided the critical lessons for what lay ahead. House No. 1 was what would later be known as "rehab in place" (or, since it was moved a stone's throw to its new perch, "rehab *almost* in place"). However, House No. 3—which had been slated for demolition and the landfill before being salvaged and moved to its new site—represented the "house rescue, move, and rehab" model that was to become the iconic Builders of Hope method.

The Cross Link Road experience provided Welsh with the crucial tools she needed, giving her the knowledge and confidence to move forward. During those six months on the job site in 2005, she was able to see the big picture of new construction—how all the moving parts fit together. She had overseen and pitched in on the prefab house, using new materials. She had worked on the two older homes as they were moved, renovated, and made ready for sale.

"Never ask anyone to do something you're not willing to do yourself."

—Nancy Welsh

Executive in Training: No Job beneath Her

As with her previous jobs in the world of business and her experience in managing a household of six, Welsh found that construction tapped her executive abilities, calling on a multitude of talents ranging from logistics to negotiation to sweet-talking to using a firm hand at times. At the end of the day, she understood that she was good at bringing all the different players together and coordinating a plan of action. Though she knew she would assume the role of chief executive in any organization she would ultimately create, she nonetheless made a point of learning every task, no matter how humble, from sanding windowsills to scraping the residue where an old commode had stood to going out for burgers and fries. "I always say, 'Never ask anyone to do something you're not willing to do yourself,'" she says.

Welsh also came to see that construction work used both sides of her brain. "For me, this field represents the perfect combination of left-brain and right-brain skills, creativity and rational thinking. You have to use your math skills to figure your budget and to calculate the height of the stair risers. How many treads do you need to make this work and fit into this limited space? At the same time, you have to be creative, to make all the pieces of the puzzle fit together, especially with rehab."

Turning Stereotypes on Edge

Another major insight for Welsh was realizing that any stereotypes she may have harbored about the construction field and its workers were false and unfounded. "It's an industry that many people don't have respect for," she says. "It's commonly considered to be populated with those who can't make it anywhere else. But that's so far from the truth. You have to be smart, resourceful, and adaptable to make it. There are codes to memorize and so many situations to deal with, from the weather to your clients to city hall." If anything, rehab requires even more ingenuity than new construction. Every rehab brings new challenges. "You might tear out sheetrock and run into mold," she says. "You might find floors that are uneven and have to figure out how to handle that."

Marketing Cross Link Road

At the outset, Welsh made the assumption that offering high-quality, affordably priced housing with a great, close-in location would bring a flock of buyers. What she didn't anticipate was having trouble selling not-so-big dream homes. Welsh quickly learned it was extremely difficult to attract new residents to lower-income sections of town. "When you perform rehab in these communities, you have to market to people who already live there," she says. "It's incredibly hard to attract newcomers into these neighborhoods—no matter how close they are to downtown, how wonderful the house is, or how reasonable the price point." This insight birthed the realization that the very families in need of new, healthy housing were the people who had been living in such neighborhoods all along.

Because the Cross Link Road project was set up on a for-profit basis, Welsh forecast selling the houses for more than she had invested in them. As a start-up, she would need to make a profit in order to evolve her venture into a viable business. The results were mixed. She did manage to sell House No. 1 on a fluke to buyers from Boston. But while House No. 2, the prefab, was on a par with, if not superior to, a brand-new stick-built home in terms of quality, buyers and agents were skeptical about its fundamentals. And though House No. 3, with its reasonable price and incredible quality, was shown frequently, no interested parties had the resources to place a successful bid. At the end of the day, Welsh was able to identify neighborhood residents who wanted Houses No. 2 and 3 but didn't qualify for bank loans.

"These last two houses went to locals who had previously been renting," she says. The only way Welsh could help get the families into the houses was by providing owner financing through lease-to-own programs. While she didn't make a fortune on her investment, she didn't lose her shirt either.

Far from being deterred by the mixed results, Welsh was energized by her foray into construction—especially the rehab component. Foremost on her mind was the existence of a huge inventory of teardown houses in Raleigh. Many of them were of excellent quality—stout and strong, some framed with old-growth timber, most more solidly built than the new structures replacing them. "They built better back then," John Jenkins says succinctly, referring to conventional wisdom about the building materials and methods of times past.

Even those issuing and carrying out the "execution orders" for teardown homes often felt remorse. Without question, many older homes were treasures that owners, developers, and house movers didn't wish to destroy. The problem was, quite simply, that they didn't know what to do with them. Recognizing the tremendous resources at hand—rich in materials and embodied energy—Welsh's creative mind started turning over the idea of performing rescue-and-rehab work to create work-force housing for families like the ones who had moved into her Cross Link Road homes.

Divine Inspiration: "A neighborhood of misfit homes"

One day in April 2006, just as she was pulling out of her neighborhood to head back for a final visit to the Cross Link Road property, Welsh had a vision. "As crazy as it sounds to build a neighborhood of misfit homes, that's what came to me. We could take not one, not two of these teardowns, but dozens of them, rehab them, and turn them into work-force housing." Welsh actually calls the moment when the idea found her "one of divine inspiration, even divine intervention. At that moment, I felt a raining down of confidence. 'This is it. It's right in front of me. God has given me the means to act upon this. If He is for me, who could be against me? This is what I'm supposed to do.'"

Sure, a huge amount of work stood between that vision and the reality of constructing a neighborhood of outdated, misshapen, and in some cases pint-sized homes. Welsh would have to work out the particulars. She would have to find and acquire the land, identify the houses, arrange to have them moved, rehab them, and sell them. She would have to assemble a team and create a process that made sense economically, environmentally, and socially. She didn't know at that moment exactly how it would happen—how she would move from Point A of her vision to Point B of making it a reality. But she had every confidence that she could do it and *would* do it.

Following her epiphany in the car, Nancy Welsh knew she had found the idea she had been looking for her entire life, the vehicle for making a difference in the world. The concept would allow her to be an agent of positive change, to act on her faith. At the same time, the entrepreneur in her understood that her crazy idea of rescuing and rehabbing teardown houses to create new neighborhoods was something, to her knowledge, that no one else in America was doing—at least not on any scale. She felt in her bones that her idea was big. What she did not know at the time was that the model she would ultimately create stood to revolutionize the world of affordable housing.

Growing Up with Boys

Nancy Lynne Welsh was born January 22, 1967, in Huntsville, Alabama, the middle child and only daughter of Dennie Martin Welsh and Jacqueline Paschke Welsh. Sandwiched between an older brother, Steve, and a younger brother, David, she grew up in the proverbial all-American family with a strong patriarchal father and a traditional stay-at-home mother. She enjoyed playing with dolls at a young age but also gravitated toward outdoor play with her brothers.

A tomboy even as a toddler, Nancy takes the helm of her uncle Ralph's tractor mower at the Fourth of July family gathering, 1969.

Welsh recalls with a chuckle that she took a greater interest in building additions to her Barbies' houses than in changing their outfits and accessories. "I would stack books to make walls," she recalls. She remembers constructing elaborate mansions on multiple levels, with nooks and crannies in which various members of Barbie's extended family of Ken, Midge, Alan, and Skipper could live, work, and play.

A playful Nancy poses in a winter hat, 1971.

In her heart of hearts, the young Nancy was an athletic, rough-and-tumble tomboy, always striving to gain acceptance from her brothers and their friends. "One of the keys to knowing me is the fact that I grew up with boys," she says. "I always felt like one of the boys."

Jackie Welsh with her children, David, Steve, and Nancy, 1973

Building Forts

When Nancy was eight, the Welsh family moved from Alabama to Cocoa, Florida, where they lived in a suburban area that bordered orange-grove country. Some of her earliest memories there involve building tree forts with Steve. Her brother's construction projects were often rather elaborate. Once, he built a two-story tree house complete with platforms and ladders. Another creation was a ground-level fort that he built right into the backyard fence. Like the tree house, it had two levels "with hatches allowing the children to bomb opponents with rotten oranges," Welsh remembers. The "opponents" were generally neighbor boys, one of whom was a redhead named Scotty Thompson, who would later make his name as the comedian Carrot Top.

The fort was made from wood scraps, chicken wire, screen, and other items. It had lights, a "red alert" (a flashing red light with a buzzer that could be activated to show that the fort was under attack), and an interior, overhead dome light so the children could play inside at night. Steve took care of the electrical end. Nancy handled the hammering.

When Nancy was around 12, Steve challenged her to a game of chicken on bicycles, the object of which was to see which sibling would "chicken out" first. The two would square off and sprint toward each other to determine the victor. Steve assumed he would win the showdown, establishing his supremacy among his siblings once and for all. In this, he severely misjudged his headstrong younger sister.

The instant Nancy accepted Steve's challenge, she made up her mind that, no matter what, she would not be the one to back down. And so the inevitable happened. Their bicycles collided head on, the handlebars hitting each of them hard. "He thought that since I was the girl, I would chicken out," Welsh says. "But I didn't. I wouldn't. I was tougher than that." In fact, her favorite T-shirt growing up was one that proclaimed, "Anything boys can do, girls can do better."

School Days: "Nancy with the Smiling Face"

At school, Nancy excelled equally in academics and athletics. She worked diligently at the tasks set before her and was popular with students and teachers alike. She was what was called "well rounded." Her radiant personality even attracted the attention of her elementary-school principal in Cocoa, who gave her the nickname "Nancy with the Smiling Face."

"Nancy with the Smiling Face" wearing a favorite hand-me-down dress from cousin Cindy, 1975

In addition to her desire to excel and please, Nancy had an equally strong need to lead. In school, she ran for almost every office that came open, and won most of them. Her election as president of TOTS (Teachers of Tomorrow's Schools) when she was in the fifth grade represented her first real leadership position with grown-up responsibilities. Among other duties, Nancy was in charge of the daily announcements, which she read over the intercom. Her early record of excelling among her peers would follow her throughout her school years and into adult life.

Her Father's Influence

To say that Nancy Welsh was influenced by her father would be an understatement. A self-made man with an up-by-the-bootstraps personal narrative, Dennie Welsh had a strong moral compass and an even stronger will. Like the woman Nancy was destined to become, her father was disciplined, driven, and principled. Welsh remembers him as being an accomplished businessman who was "impressively articulate and visionary," a leader who served as a role model for his three children.

Though there was never any question that her father ruled the roost, her mother was "the glue that held it all together," Welsh remembers. "Dad was boss and the final authority. He made all the decisions—from the large ones like where we would live and how to raise the children to the small ones like where to go to dinner." But her mother was "the quiet strength that he counted on." She chuckles in recalling a line from the film *My Big Fat Greek Wedding*: "The man is the head, but the woman is the neck. And she can turn the head any way she wants." "That sums up my parents' relationship," she says. When Dennie Welsh passed away at the age of 61 in 2004, Welsh remembers her mother being completely devastated.

Humble Beginnings

Nancy Welsh's parents grew up poor in Fayetteville, Tennessee, a small town in the south-central part of the state near the Alabama line. Her father was an only child. "My father's first home was a rented bedroom in someone's house," she says. "Dad used to joke that the reason he never had brothers or sisters was because he had to sleep in his parents' room."

Nancy's paternal grandparents, Ada and Clifford Welsh, flank her great-grandmother Elizabeth Welsh after church in Fayetteville, Tennessee, 1963.

An intense, gifted boy with an agile mind, strong people skills, and an innate entrepreneurial spirit, Dennie Welsh modeled himself after his uncle Ralph, the principal at the elementary school he attended, where his own father held the job of janitor. His mother supplemented the family income as a part-time clerk in the jewelry store on the town square. As was common in the 1940s and 1950s, young Dennie started working as a child. In the summertime, he walked or rode his bike a couple of miles out to the fields to pick cotton all day, carrying his lunch and thermos in his basket. He learned the habit of thrift early, saving every nickel he could for the future. His only indulgence with his childhood earnings was going to the movies on weekends.

Dennie Welsh's school photo, 1954

The Sadie Hawkins Dance

Jacqueline Paschke had a similar hardscrabble upbringing. If anything, hers was even tougher. Her biological father—a war veteran and regionally famous singer—died when she was just five years old. Her mother remarried not long after, and the young Jackie was

Jackie Paschke in her ball gown before her high-school dance

subsequently saddled with the responsibility of helping rear three younger stepsiblings when her mother went into factory work to make ends meet. Those early responsibilities and challenges molded Jackie's character, endowing her with a confidence beyond her years. It was she who initiated the relationship with her future husband. Welsh's mother was in the eighth grade when she invited Dennie Welsh, a year older, out on their first date, to a Sadie Hawkins dance. Dennie accepted, and the two soon became inseparable.

After graduating from high school in 1960, Dennie Welsh enrolled in Middle Tennessee State University in nearby Murfreesboro on an Army ROTC scholarship. Jackie Paschke followed a year later and attended summer school to catch up with her steady beau. Dennie took a job in the cafeteria and quickly emerged as a campus leader, winning election as class president his freshman year. Jackie, a pretty and popular student who loved to sing, was named May Queen her senior year. Upon graduating with a degree in mathematics in 1964, Dennie went to work for the United States Army's First Air Defense Guided Missile Brigade at Fort Bliss in El Paso, Texas. Jackie also graduated in 1964, with degrees in English and secondary teaching. She completed four years of college in just three while also holding down a job in the university's Admissions Office. The young couple tied the knot just after graduation.

Jackie was a hardworking student at Middle Tennessee State University. She graduated with a four-year degree in just three years.

Dennie Welsh, far left, *with other student leaders at Middle Tennessee State University. He served as vice chairman of the Southern Universities Student Government Association and was voted "Most Versatile Senior Boy."*

The Company Man

In 1967, after completing his army stint, Dennie Welsh was recruited to work for IBM as a programmer on the company's space initiative, the objective of which was to put a man on the moon by the end of the decade. He rose rapidly through the ranks of Big Blue and worked for the company his entire career. In the 1980s, as an IBM vice president, Dennie created and ran the company's Integrated Systems Solutions Corporation (ISSC). The division did pioneering work in the field that came to be known as "information technology." In 1995, Welsh was tapped to be the first-ever general manager of what became IBM's Global Services Division. In his book, *Who Says Elephants Can't Dance? Inside IBM's Historic Turnaround*, former CEO Lou Gerstner credits the work of Dennie Welsh with the company's revival.

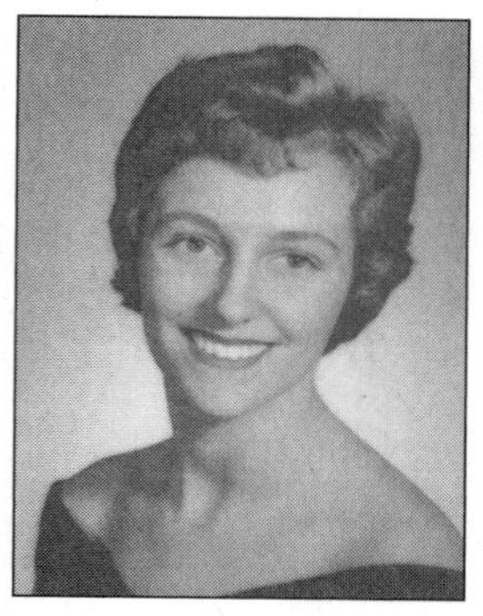

The beautiful Jackie Paschke was voted May Queen her senior year in college.

Dennie and Jackie tied the knot in July 1964 in Fayetteville, Tennessee.

Nancy Welsh was always moved by her mother's warm heart, graceful servitude, and strong Christian faith—traits carried through to Nancy's personality and work to this day. From her father, Welsh learned lessons about how to conduct herself in work, about doing the right thing, and about how to succeed in business. "Dad was a fast learner. He was responsive to what people wanted. He would go out and listen to his customers and figure out what they needed."

Welsh was also impressed by her father's work ethic. He was honest and cared about others on his team. She remembers him working around the clock, traveling constantly, and even holding business meetings on airplanes. When he was home, he worked into the wee hours and was always up at the crack of dawn, a

Colonel Harkins pins bars for promotion on Dennie as Jackie looks on.

IDENTIFICATION:

Dennie M. Welsh
6346 B Morgan Road
Fort Bliss, Texas 79906

Telephone 915 772-7256

CAREER OBJECTIVE:
To initiate my career in personnel management or industrial relations leading to a future managerial position.

SUMMARY OF QUALIFICATIONS:
For the past ten months have been Assistant Operations Officer responsible for the training and evaluation of 850-1100 students per month at an Army Training Center. Employed by the student personnel office my senior year in college to supervise a men's dormitory. Worked with student government throughout college career.

WORK EXPERIENCE:
During the summers 1961-62-63 worked for Tennessee Department of Highways surveying and acquiring right of way for the interstate highway system. Worked twenty hours per week throughout college career in college cafeteria. Worked weekends in men's clothing store.

MILITARY SERVICE:
Upon graduation from college was commissioned a Second Lieutenant in the United States Army and assigned to Fort Bliss, Texas for two years active duty. Completed the Air Defense Officers Orientation Course and was assigned as platoon leader for seven months, then to the Group Commander's staff as Assistant Operations Officer, S-3, the position now held. Scheduled to be released from active duty July 23, 1966, and will revert to a two year reserve status. Available for employment immediately upon release from active duty.

EDUCATION:
Received B.S. in mathematics from Middle Tennessee State University, Murfreesboro, Tennessee, May 1964. Minor courses of study were industrial arts and secondary education. Overall grade point ratio 2.6. Ninety percent of total college expenses financed through summer and part-time jobs; ten percent by parental support. Campus honors: various honorary fraternities, club offices, Freshman class president, student congress member, Attorney General for student government, Most Versatile Senior Boy, Vice Chairman, Southern Universities Student Government Association.

PERSONAL DATA:
Date of birth-December 30, 1942; height-5'9½"; weight-180 pounds; martial status-married; dependents-3; physical limitations-none.

REFERENCES:
References will be furnished upon request by the applicant or from the Placement Office, Middle Tennessee State University, Murfreesboro, Tennessee.

An early résumé of Dennie Welsh reveals his ambition and work ethic.

routine that seemed to come with the territory for upper management at a world-class organization like IBM.

Learning Frugality

Though Dennie Welsh provided his wife and family with a far more comfortable lifestyle than he had enjoyed growing up, he nonetheless wanted to impart to his children the lessons that had so powerfully motivated him in his youth. Welsh remembers the ethic of frugality threading through their family life in the 1970s. "My parents always lived *below* their means," she says. "They were great role models for financial responsibility." Her parents pinched pennies and put aside every dollar they could for the future. When she was in grade school, her mother sewed much of her clothing, Welsh remembers. When her mother did buy her daughter ready-made items, she would inevitably take her shopping at "very practical places" like Sears and J. C. Penney.

Summer vacations were an important ritual in the Welsh family. One of Dennie's ambitions was to visit every state, and though they didn't quite make it, they covered a lot of ground. Every summer, they would load up the station wagon and hit the road. Welsh remembers her parents packing in large quantities of food—cereal, crackers, Spam, cans of beans and corn. "Many nights, we'd have Spam and eggs for dinner, or pinto beans and mashed potatoes, and we'd sleep in the car." Her father worked so hard that just having his undivided attention made those times stand out. Many of Welsh's happiest childhood memories come from those simple times together.

Jackie Welsh loads up the family camper and her children, 1969.

Langley High track star Nancy Welsh poses with her winning mile relay team, 1984.

Tame Teen Years

When Nancy was 12, the family moved from Florida to Northern Virginia, and she left behind the orange groves for life in the fast lane. That fall, she entered the seventh grade at Cooper Intermediate School in McLean. Two years later, she enrolled in the prestigious and ultra-competitive Langley High School, a tony public school that enrolled the children of Washington's political elite. Ian Brzezinski, son of former Carter administration national security advisor Zbigniew Brzezinski, was one of many noteworthy students there. Nancy quickly made a name at Langley, establishing herself in sports, in academics, and as a student leader. In fact, the young Brzezinski escorted the beautiful blond freshman to the senior prom.

Nancy filled her schedule with school activities and church life and always worked hard to live up to her parents' expectations. "I never smoked a cigarette or took drugs like so many of my peers did," she recalls. "Even if I'd wanted to, which I didn't, I wouldn't dare risk the wrath of my father."

In junior high, Nancy babysat regularly. At age 14, she went to work selling Avon products door to door. "I quickly learned that in business, time is money," she recalls. "So while I enjoyed

Nancy, Steve, and David at home in McLean, Virginia, 1985

talking with the older ladies I called on, I tried to devise ways to prevent 45-minute conversations for the purchase of a tube of lipstick that would net me 50 cents or a dollar profit." Her strategy was to have samples at the ready so she could turn the conversation around the product from the get-go. By her junior year in high school, she landed a part-time office job at a head-hunting agency, Paul-Tittle and Associates. In the summers, she always worked full time in order to afford the designer jeans that the other girls wore.

Harvard University: "No thanks. Not for my daughter."

Nancy admits to becoming increasingly skeptical about her father's tight control over her life during those years. Nothing drove the point home more clearly than an incident during her senior year at Langley High School. A top student, Nancy was president of the student body and lettered in three varsity sports. At her graduation, she won the outstanding citizenship award from the Kiwanis Club and the top leadership award from B'nai Brith, among other honors. But when an admissions officer from Harvard University visited the school wanting to recruit her, her father refused to allow her to even fill out an application. He viewed Harvard as too expensive, too Yankee, and too liberal for his daughter. Better, he said, that Nancy return to his native Tennessee to further her education. It had, after all, been good enough for him, and it would serve her well, too.

Nancy, home on break from college, and her father share a happy moment, 1986.

Wrestling down her disappointment over the Ivy League education that was not to be, Nancy buckled under and followed her father's directive. In the fall of 1985, she enrolled in the University of Tennessee at Knoxville. Straightaway, she went to work at the college cafeteria to earn spending money, as her father had done two decades before at Middle Tennessee State. She threw herself into campus life, becoming a resident assistant, a Student Government Association representative, and vice president of the Residence Hall Association. When Coca-Cola products were removed from campus vending machines and replaced with Pepsi, Nancy started a petition drive and worked with the news media to reinstate them. "Within six weeks, we had Coke back on campus."

Along with her best friend, Mary Schinbeckler, a fellow RA from Cookeville, Tennessee, Nancy enjoyed spreading good cheer in their residence hall and creating greeting-card-like slogans to fit many occasions—cheery verses to congratulate, to celebrate, to egg on, or to try to lift the spirits of someone who was ill or who had suffered heartbreak. Sometimes they wrote ditties on cards; sometimes they posted them on the wall. The two girls had so much fun with their hobby that they seriously entertained the idea of starting their own greeting-card company once they got out into the real world.

First Job, Then Marriage

Nancy Welsh graduated from the University of Tennessee in 1989 as an advertising major with a degree in communications. She initially accepted a job offer from American Greetings. Back home in McLean, as she awaited the assignment of her sales territory, she grew impatient. In hindsight, she realizes she may have waited no more than a week or two. But at the time, it seemed like a lifetime for a young woman in a hurry to make her mark in the world of work. Rather than wait it out, she decided to renew a previous application with Coca-Cola USA. Over 100 applicants put in for the job, but by working her magic on the interview team—trotting out her fight to save Coke on the University of Tennessee campus couldn't have hurt—the young woman beat out the competition and won the plum position. What's more, she was awarded the sales territory she had her eye on: Northern Virginia.

Welsh tapped her considerable people skills to advance rapidly. She loved the challenge of figuring out how to become a successful salesperson. As her father had done so effectively with his clients, Welsh drove the area calling on managers at fast-food restaurants and convenience stores to get to know their needs and their hot buttons. She put on her listening cap to figure out how to motivate different buyers, devising a customized strategy for each one. Her methods worked, and she drastically increased sales.

In her personal life, Welsh once again looked to her parents' example. Following in their footsteps, she married young, tying the knot with the man with whom she had palled around in college, Avern Leslie "Les" Murray III. After six months on the job for Coca-Cola, Nancy married Les on December 16, 1989. Their first child, Benjamin Chase, was born in 1991, followed by two more boys—Jack Christian, born in 1994, and Austin Cole, born in 1999. In October 2001, they completed their family with the adoption of their daughter, Anastasia Joy, a six-year-old orphan from Kazakhstan.

Standing Her Ground: "I'm having a baby. You can still promote me."

At Coca-Cola, Nancy Welsh learned effective sales strategies. But just as importantly, she learned how to fend for herself on the job. In the male-chauvinist work environment that was Coca-Cola, she realized it was up to her to demand appropriate compensation to match her impressive accomplishments. At the time she was pregnant with her first child, her manager expressed his skepticism that she would keep her job once she gave birth. "He said, 'You're going to be breast-feeding a baby with one hand and driving with the other,'" she distinctly recalls. Her boss refused to give her the raise she knew was due her.

Instead of sitting back, nursing a grudge, or taking potshots at her manager, she sprang into action in characteristic Nancy Welsh style. Quite simply, she went over the man's head and approached the area vice president to make her case. "I sat him down and said, 'I'm having a baby. You can still promote me.' I went right to the numbers. I had the highest number of conversions from Pepsi to Coke of any sales rep in the state, and the highest number of sales." In the end, Welsh got her pay raise and her promotion. She also realized that she had to hold her ground—that no one was going to hand success to her. "Women at Coca-Cola had to work five times as hard as the guys just to be on the same footing," she says.

Working on the Kellogg's Account: "I'm all in"

After six years on the job for Coca-Cola, Welsh realized she needed a new challenge and decided to have a go at the field she had studied in college: advertising. She always had a way of starting at the top. After just a few months of looking, she landed an interview and then a job with the international advertising powerhouse Leo Burnett, working out of company headquarters in Chicago. Leo Burnett executives quickly realized their young hire's potential and assigned her the account for an exploding new business: the single-serve cereal products sold to institutions, hotels, and vending machines by Kellogg's, a major client. As fate would have it, she was ready for the challenge from day one, having written her senior thesis in college on the Kellogg's approach to new product launches.

At the time she was given the account, Leo Burnett "didn't know what to do with this business," Welsh recalls. Her supervisors brought her in to be the "fix-it person." Just as she had accepted her brother's challenge to play chicken on wheels 15 years

Sons Ben and Jack cuddle with Nancy on a fall evening in 1998 at Nancy's parents' home in Williamsburg, Virginia.

earlier, she took on the challenge with every intention of succeeding. "I'm the kind of person who, when I get into something, I'm all in," she says. "I exploded their ad business, taking something they thought was impossible to do and made it go. I tripled their ad business in two years in the Away from Home Consumption division."

Her secret? Once again, Welsh tapped into the power of human potential, using a team approach in an industry that too often got tripped up by dueling egos and personalities. Where animosity among clients, client services, and the creative team had existed in the past, Nancy with the Smiling Face managed to pull together a united front. "I took the creative guy and made him a part of the client team. I'd bring him to client meetings." By the same token, instead of "handling" clients by holding them at arm's-length as the "creatives" so often did, Welsh realized that if she brought them into the process of creating and developing ad campaigns, heard their ideas out, and allowed them to have input, selling the final ad product would be a piece of cake. To that end, she was always quick to give credit to others—especially clients—for the ideas that surfaced in brainstorming sessions. "'What a great idea,' I'd say. 'Way to go! You should have my job.'" Using her common-sense, feel-good approach helped bring great ideas to the surface, created buy-in, and paved the way to successful campaigns. "Everything in life," she realized then, "is sales."

Once she proved herself, the company expanded her Kellogg's territory to include Canada—a huge account that carried tremendous opportunities for growth and reward. When Welsh's husband was transferred to Raleigh, North Carolina, Leo Burnett realized she was too valuable to lose, so the company made special arrangements for her to work from a distance. From her base in Raleigh, she set up a home office and commuted regularly to Chicago and Battle Creek, Michigan.

But just when it seemed she was headed toward a lifelong career in advertising, Welsh's path again took a sharp turn.

Living Simply in the Outback

In 1999, her husband received a job transfer to Sydney, Australia. With a baby in diapers and two young boys, Welsh decided to

Stay-at-home mom Nancy with her three boys in Sydney, Australia. Baby Austin peeks out from Mom's arm.

take a break from her career and devote herself to mothering full time. She and her family were in Australia only a little over a year, but the time away had a powerful and profound impact on the evolution of her thinking. Living outside the bubble of American culture had the effect of putting her in closer touch with how the rest of the world lived.

One of the most striking observations Welsh made in the Harbour City was how many fewer possessions the Aussies had than her fellow Americans back home. The Welsh house in Sydney was only slightly smaller than the one in North Carolina, but the relative paucity of possessions was a significant difference.

Baby Austin, age one, on a couch in Sydney, Australia, 2000

The family had left more than half of their household possessions behind. Initially, their Australian home seemed "almost empty without all of the stuff we had left behind," Welsh recalls. But she quickly noticed that the possessions they had put in mothballs were largely unnecessary and quickly forgotten and that, rather than being compromised, their lifestyle benefited as a result. They lived more simply and with less stress. The children spent more time playing outdoors, and the family participated more regularly in community and school activities. "Somehow, not having so much stuff—toys, computer games, home movies—there was less to take care of, to clean up, and to otherwise occupy our time."

Possession Overload

When the family returned to Raleigh in November 2000 and found their boatload of possessions awaiting them, Welsh was not

Jackie and Nancy celebrate Nancy's birthday in Sydney, Australia, 2000.

happy to reclaim her old things but instead felt "overwhelmed and saddened" to see all of them. She was burdened by their weight.

Stepping away from the materialistic lifestyle of North America, she started doing some big-picture thinking: Why did Americans work so hard to acquire so many things and devote themselves to amassing personal fortunes, often at the expense of their families and health? It struck her that their treadmill did not make them any happier. The period in Australia—which amounted to a kind of sabbatical for Welsh—was a time of personal reflection about values and faith. Were the Americans she was spending time with leading lives of service to humanity? To God?

New Beginnings: The Tug of Public Service

Back in Raleigh, Welsh was a new person. She continued to stay home with the kids and felt her desire to climb the corporate ladder and make boatloads of money fading away. At the same time, something new was taking root inside her: the desire to make a significant difference in the world.

Nancy and daughter Anna enjoy a family vacation in the Florida Keys, 2009.

After the yearlong adoption process of her then six-year-old daughter was complete, Welsh decided to get involved with local government, focusing on the growth of the city of Raleigh and its impact on neighborhoods, schools, and such issues as water supply. She signed on to the Citizens' Advisory Council (CAC), the entity that handled zoning recommendations for residential construction and subdivisions. In 2005, she was elected cochair of the CAC, a position she held for two years. Though she didn't know it at the time, her community work was setting the stage and giving her valuable experience for the endeavor she would soon birth.

Starting Builders of Hope

After her epiphany in the car about creating a community of misfit homes, Nancy Welsh set to work figuring out how to make it happen. She had walked away from her foray into the Cross Link Road development with valuable lessons about house moving, rehab, and marketing in a distressed inner-city community. Welsh was also aware that success in business was largely equated with the bottom line. And while she had just broken even on Cross Link Road, she nonetheless believed the entire experience had been a success.

Her mind kept coming back to the resources that were wasted with teardowns—good, sturdy housing stock that could form the basis of perfectly decent homes. While she had saved two houses, she knew that many, many more were out there waiting to be rescued. Most, though not all, of the teardowns were out of date and would not perform well against new construction in the mainstream residential housing marketplace. Based on her experience at Cross Link Road, she realized that a for-profit operation could not make enough money to remain afloat by selling such properties in the neighborhoods that needed them most.

But for a *nonprofit*, the idea just might fly. Doing such work as a nonprofit organization would allow her to drive the costs lower—to get breaks in pricing, donations, awards, and grants that could turn the operation into a viable charitable enterprise. And it would make the houses even more affordable. Welsh ran the idea past her accountant and attorney. It didn't take long for her to understand that she was onto something.

After polling advisors whose opinions mattered to her, Welsh took stock of her resources. Her father had died in 2004, and although most of his fortune was tied up in estate trusts, he had left each of his children enough money to underwrite something serious. Rather than let her share of that money languish in stocks and earn dividends, Welsh decided she'd like to put it to work. "I wanted to do something to make a difference to others," she says.

In 2006, she sent off the papers establishing a nonprofit organization called Builders of Hope as a 501(c)(3), with a board of directors and provisional tax-exempt status. With each step she took, she did more digging about the social and economic landscape in America for people less privileged than herself. That research brought her face to face with the enormous void of affordable housing for a large number of people. Those people were not destitute. Rather, they were the working middle class—teachers, policemen, secretaries, those in service and retail jobs. In founding Builders of Hope, Welsh was not only creating a new model but gaining insight about—and a passion to improve and reform—fundamental social, economic, and quality-of-life conditions in the United States.

CHAPTER 2

AFFORDABLE HOUSING IN AMERICA: A CALL TO ACTION

Economic, social, and environmental issues and conditions all contribute to the failure of the current mode of urban redevelopment and to the nation's inability to adequately provide affordable housing to Americans, including those who make up the majority of the work force—the struggling middle class, the working poor, and those living in poverty. This overview of the affordable housing landscape in the United States identifies pressing national concerns that underscore the need for a fundamental shift in the preservation and development of affordable housing. Tearing down existing properties to make way for new construction is simply too costly—environmentally, economically, and socially—to continue to prevail. It is an urgent national priority that this way of doing business be retired, so that better models can be embraced.

Teardown: The Old Way

After her initial foray into construction in Raleigh, North Carolina, Nancy Welsh quickly perceived the inherent value in teardown houses, which inspired the creation of Builders of Hope. Leery of tearing down structures, she was more concerned about what was lost than the blank slate that had been gained.

A recent headline in the *Winston-Salem* (North Carolina) *Journal* told a story that is all too common in America. "Tumbled Down," read the headline. The cutline explained, "Arts school tears down 3 houses in historic area." The lead story on the front page of the local news section, the article displayed three full-color photos of houses on the chopping block arranged around the featured player—a bulldozer as it trained its powerful force on a partially demolished home. The tone of the article seemed to celebrate the demise of the three homes as if it were a sign of victory, of the progress of man. And yet the photos of the homes told another story. They reached out to readers not unlike those shots of unlucky, forlorn pets up for adoption, whom everyone knows will meet their maker if no one steps forward in short order to claim them.

One of the photos of the houses in the historic Centerville neighborhood adjacent to downtown Winston-Salem showed a darling Victorian gingerbread behind a neatly manicured lawn. The second appeared to be a solid rancher with a brick façade. The third was a modest but sturdy wood-frame home with the remnants of what appeared to be a large and inviting front porch. The histories of the homes and the people they had nurtured through the years vanished on that day.

The date of the article—May 25, 2010—was arresting because it was so recent. Arresting, too, was the agency issuing the order. It was not some bottom-line-driven corporation or a government entity seeking highway or infrastructure expansion. Instead, the wrecking ball was summoned by none other than a state arts school, which apparently had no immediate plan for the land other than to clear it for some future, but as yet undesignated, use.

The associate vice chancellor for facilities management told the newspaper that the school was in the process of "revamping its master plan" and "so far has no concrete plans for the lots." The arts school representative stated that the houses to be razed were in "extremely poor condition" and went on to note the presence of asbestos. "With our high school population, removal of asbestos is a high priority," he said.

Well, yes, asbestos can pose a problem, but only when "friable" or airborne, as when particles are released in a structure that is undergoing renovation. This would affect not only high schoolers but every age group inhaling this known carcinogen. Further, the presence of asbestos did not demand the structures' immediate demolition. It could have been contained through encapsulation. It might have been professionally remediated or removed. In either case, the asbestos had to be dealt with prior to tearing down the homes. Condemning them for the mere presence of asbestos smacked of justification-seeking rather than bona fide reasoning.

What the arts school representative did *not* address in the *Winston-Salem Journal* report was the myriad costs associated with tearing down. Those included hard costs—the cost of abatement for asbestos and lead prior to demolition, the money spent on the demolition itself, the cost of removing the building material, the cost of trucking off debris and adding it to already-overflowing landfills. Nor did the school's calculation account for the environmental cost—what is commonly referred to as the "carbon cost"—of the materials destroyed, which were rich in resources and embodied energy.

And the school representative did not speak to the loss of housing stock, especially at the affordable level. The people displaced by teardowns such as these have to live somewhere. They have to search for housing and then make the physical move. The cost of displacement involves time, money, and effort. And finally, the last cost of the three houses fell under the amorphous umbrella of historical, cultural, and social value. Each home was a visual piece of the cultural fabric of the community. Each was a link—a bit player, to take a page out of the arts school's own playbook—in the overall architectural production of the neighborhood.

An "Epidemic" of Teardowns

"That's okay because I expect to tear this one down in 20 years."

—New Jersey builder, challenged to defend the fact that the house he was tearing down was more solidly built than the one he was replacing it with

Earlier in the first decade of the new millennium, the National Trust for Historic Preservation identified what it called a "teardown epidemic" that was raging through the nation and wiping out historic neighborhoods "one house at a time." The congressionally chartered organization, founded in 1949, pinpointed the teardown crisis as one of grave national concern and offered significant resources to householders, community activists, preservationists, and other stakeholders to fight the trend. "As older homes are demolished and replaced with dramatically larger, out-of-scale new structures, the historic character of the existing neighborhood is changed forever," the National Trust's website states under the heading, "Teardowns and McMansions." The page goes on to address the diminution of neighborhood livability "as trees are removed, backyards are eliminated, and sunlight is blocked by towering new structures built up to the property lines. Community economic and social diversity is reduced as new mansions replace affordable homes."

Though the economic downturn of the latter part of the decade slowed the voluntary destruction of properties to be replaced by new construction, many homes nonetheless continued to fall victim to the wrecking ball, whether by teardown, eminent domain, or other means. "Certainly, we've seen in some markets around the country a slowdown of teardowns," says Adrian Scott Fine, director of state and local policy for the National Trust. "In other markets such as Dallas or Austin, we're still seeing them happen, [though] maybe not at the same pace as two or three years ago." Despite this slowdown, Fine predicts that "teardowns are not likely to go away." He recounts with chagrin the response of a New Jersey builder who was challenged to defend the fact that the house he was tearing down was more solidly built than the one he was replacing it with. The builder responded, "That's okay because I expect to tear this one down in 20 years." The comment has become legend around the National Trust office.

Though tearing down houses and replacing them with grander structures is hardly new, experts say that the trend took off in the mid- to late 1990s and reached a peak during the house-building boom years of 2004 to early 2007. The National Trust stepped in to document and combat teardowns when its leaders realized the problem was spreading beyond isolated resort and high-wealth communities. "When we started in 2002, we did quantify 100 communities in 20 states that were dealing with significant teardown," Fine says. "When we last updated the numbers in 2008, we identified 400 communities in 40 states."

"One of the problems underlying the teardown phenomenon is out-of-date, bad zoning. The solution is better zoning."

—Jim Lindberg, National Trust for Historic Preservation

National numbers documenting the teardown of functioning, habitable houses are hard to come by because communities have such divergent means of recordkeeping. Derelict, abandoned, and falling-down houses inhabit one category, while functional, habitable homes inhabit another. Some communities such as Denver do an excellent job tracking teardown numbers, in part because the city's leaders understand the issue and are working to slow, if not stop, the phenomenon. In 2007, for instance, almost 800 structures (a figure that combines both functional and dilapidated housing, along with other buildings) in Denver were torn down to make way for new construction, says Jim Lindberg, director of preservation initiatives for the Mountains/Plains office of the National Trust. That number dropped dramatically, to a projected 250 teardowns in the city for 2010.

"One of the problems underlying the teardown phenomenon is out-of-date, bad zoning," Lindberg says. "The solution is better zoning." While zoning is not a panacea and doesn't always provide solutions, it can be an excellent tool and starting point. In June 2010, Denver passed what Lindberg calls a "context-sensitive, form-based zoning code," which started with an analysis of existing patterns. The process takes into account where buildings are sited on lots and examines setbacks, the proposed buildings' scale, and the way finished properties will look in the public realm. Miami has passed a similar measure, and forward-thinking municipal planners around the nation are taking advantage of the current slow building period to revise zoning codes in advance of an anticipated recovery.

High-profile Fights over Historically Significant Homes

In years past, serious and high-profile fights were waged in communities across the nation over the preservation of homes deemed historically significant. Half a decade ago, a major battle ensued in the tony Chicago suburb of Kenilworth over the decision to tear down the famous Skiff House at 157 Kenilworth Avenue. Built in 1908 for Frederick Skiff, the visionary first director of Chicago's Field Museum of Natural History, the house was designed by one of the nation's preeminent turn-of-the-20th-century architectural firms, Daniel H. Burnham. The plan to demolish the home not long after its purchase in 2004 for just under $2 million created a community uproar, according to Daniel P. McMillen, economics professor at the University of Illinois at Chicago. The strong community reaction ultimately resulted in the private sale of the property—just days prior to its scheduled demolition—to a concerned neighbor, who handed over a hefty premium to the short-term owner.

In June 2010, another historic home met a different fate. In about an hour's time, an excavator for the city of Detroit demolished the boyhood home of former Massachusetts governor Mitt Romney, whose famous father was George W. Romney, a Republican governor of Michigan, head of American Motors Corporation, and presidential candidate, like his son. According to a report in the *Wall Street Journal*, people in the exclusive Palmer Woods neighborhood, the site of the two-story, 5,500-square-foot home, "take pride in their tradition of historic preservation." Though a few opposed its destruction, the Romney home came down as part of a larger city plan. Indeed, the same *Journal* article went on to report that the city of Detroit was "finally getting serious about razing thousands of vacant and abandoned structures across the city . . . chipping away at a glut of abandoned homes that has been piling up for decades." According to the report, Detroit mayor Dave Bing, armed with $20 million in federal funding, including stimulus dollars, had promised to tear down some 10,000 buildings during his first term in office as a central component of his plan to "right-size" the city. Some advocates of the demo plan voiced the need for a "clean slate" in order "to lower crime and help potential residents to see the opportunity instead of the blight."

Questions about the wisdom of demolishing properties on that scale—and the repercussions for the people being dislocated—apparently are either going unanswered or are not yet gaining traction.

"Instead of [house] removal aiding a healthy block process, teardown actually sets up the contagious process of destruction. It adds blight in the entire neighborhood."

—Mindy Thompson Fullilove, MD, author of *Root Shock*

Poor People's Housing: Fair Game for the Wrecking Ball

While big show houses and historically significant homes such as the Romney property and the Skiff home can stir controversy and command headlines when they're slated for demolition, the dwellings of poorer people have been traditionally considered fair game for the wrecking ball, barely even worthy of discussion. In years past, the preservation community—when forced to choose its battles—often rallied round grander homes, failing to muster the same level of energy and passion for saving affordable, lower-income, and work-force neighborhoods.

According to the National Trust's Adrian Scott Fine, the preservation community places greater emphasis on retaining "community character" than on saving major community landmarks. That may well be true, but the reality is that until the public, builders, developers, and community officials buy into the concept that smaller, less outwardly significant properties are worth saving, too, the teardown phenomenon is likely to continue unchallenged, albeit at a somewhat decelerated pace.

Why Do We Tear Down?

As a nation, we continue to operate on autopilot. In addition to the classic (and classically horrific) teardown scenario in which highly functional smaller homes are knocked down to be replaced by structures on average three times the size of the original, we are also leveling the diminishing stock of affordable work-force housing as an almost automatic first step to creating new housing in low-income and urban communities. As a result, we bulldoze blighted, foreclosed, and boarded-up properties to clear them from sight and make way for the "new and better" structures of the future. Sadly, the new structures are often more poorly constructed than their predecessors. In many instances, they are never built at all.

Why do we do it? It's a tricky question, and the answers are complex. For starters, tearing down is the way we've done it for many years. Secondly, teardowns offer a relatively quick fix, with their promise to clean up neighborhoods. Tearing down offers those seeking to transform neighborhoods the illusion that they are doing *something* in the face of the often dilapidated, outdated, or difficult-to-remediate buildings that mar the visual landscape.

The Scope of the Teardown Problem

Americans demolish some 250,000 homes annually, according to the Environmental Protection Agency. Though in recent years developers have increased efforts to salvage reusable items such as bathtubs, light figures, and mantels, mountains of demolition debris continue to clog the nation's landfills. Extrapolating from figures provided by the National Trust for Historic Preservation, tearing down a house of roughly 2,000 square feet creates, on average, around 16 tons (or 32,000 pounds) of debris. Though the amount of debris associated with each house varies widely—depending on materials, construction, location, size, and many additional factors—it is safe to say that it amounts to tens of millions of pounds in landfills annually. Numerous other costs exist as well.

Not in My Backyard: The High Cost of Landfilling

When the cost of building a new McMansion where an older brick ranch home used to be is calculated, the price tag of demolition tends to be included, along with the construction cost for the new home, but the landfill burden of the material torn down—what's referred to as "vacated landfill space"—is almost *never* figured into the equation.

In America, landfills are rapidly reaching capacity. And due to the public's understandable aversion to allowing them to be located near their homes and communities, new ones are increasingly difficult to site. Experts predict that a landfill shortage crisis will rear its ugly head in the short-term future. Public objections to siting new landfills are myriad, but the most common ones stem from the multitude of environmental and economic repercussions of packing garbage into large man-made cavities of land. Americans continue to produce mountains of trash on a daily basis. (Pre-recession figures show that, on average, every American generates 4.5 pounds of waste every day.) The solutions that are closest at hand derive from a simple saw: Reduce, reuse, and recycle. Yet despite the fact that the call to consumption reduction is not new, Americans have been slow to embrace the fundamental principle.

- Construction waste contributes roughly *30 percent* of the content of America's landfills. If the amount of waste at the front end can be reduced through recycling existing homes, citizens can make a major, impactful contribution to easing the burden on landfills.
- "Buildings—their construction and operation—account for greater than 40 percent of the United States' carbon dioxide emissions."

National Trust for Historic Preservation

Methane Gas Drives Global Warming

Our ever-expanding landfills contribute mightily to climate change. The breakdown of organic material from landfills provides the ideal conditions for methanogenesis, a process that produces methane gas and continues for years after landfills are closed. Global estimates put the methane emanating from landfills annually in the tens to hundreds of millions of tons, primarily from First World countries, which contribute the highest concentrations of waste. Methane gas drives global warming. Experts say that the levels of methane have more than doubled since the preindustrial period. Methane levels account for roughly one-fifth of the man-made contribution to greenhouse-gas-driven global warming.

In addition to the costs of landfilling, the carbon emissions associated with transporting waste from leveled homes to landfills must figure into the calculations, as must the human energy that accompanies this endeavor. But the material costs of destroying habitable homes are not the only ones. And they may not even be the most significant costs.

Urban Renewal and the Shock of Loss

When a house is torn down, the entire community experiences the loss. Houses act as both shelters for people and as significant foundational structures in the neighborhood. "The best analogy is teeth," explains Mindy Thompson Fullilove, MD, professor of clinical psychiatry and public health at Columbia University and author of *Root Shock: How Tearing Up City Neighborhoods Hurts America, and What We Can Do about It.* Fullilove draws an analogy that, once grasped, is almost impossible to forget. "It's clear to us you're *not* supposed to pull out teeth. Dentists try to preserve every single tooth they can." The same goes for houses, she says. If a house—even a vacant or boarded-up property—is brought down, the houses on either side become more vulnerable. "Instead of its removal aiding a healthy block process," Fullilove says, "teardown actually sets up the contagious process of destruction. It adds blight in the entire neighborhood."

Likewise, *the destruction of entire communities* under the urban renewal programs of the middle part of the last century not only caused serious damage to the environment and to housing capacity but also severely scarred those communities. Most of these government-backed programs were in effect from the late 1940s until the early part of the 1970s, Fullilove says.

Perhaps no one has told the story more movingly or eloquently than Mary Bishop, who in the mid-1990s wrote a path-breaking series for the *Roanoke* (Virginia) *Times and World News* chillingly documenting exactly how an African-American community was dismantled by urban renewal. Titled "Street by Street, Block by Block," the articles connected the physical demise of the neighborhood with the ensuing wholesale destruction of the community, along with its rich cultural and economic life. "Something began happening 40 years ago that changed Roanoke forever," Bishop writes in the introduction to her series, which ran in January and February 1995. "It displaced thousands of men, women and children, wiping out neighborhoods and institutions. A long chain of broken promises scarred citizens' political trust so badly that the bitterness flares up in public hearings to this day."

Bishop goes on to report how damaging federally funded urban renewal was to the black community around the city's oldest neighborhoods of Northeast Roanoke and Gainsboro. "Government leaders here thought urban renewal was a progressive way to clear what looked like slums to them and put in highways, industries and public complexes. But there was a lack of understanding among those policymakers . . . of what life was really like in black neighborhoods, what those communities meant to people, and exactly what would happen to the families made to leave. . . .

"*Slum* and *blight* are words that Roanoke's older white leaders use to describe what they saw in those neighborhoods. Black people who lived there had another word for it: *Home*. . . . Gainsboro natives still argue among themselves about whether they should have fought harder against urban renewal, which promised revival of one of the city's oldest neighborhoods but wound up doing more tearing down than building up."

The executive director of a local antipoverty agency shared with Bishop's readers the long-lasting impacts of urban renewal on the community. "These actions have for decades left the impression that the City of Roanoke not only has no regard for black neighborhoods and their institutions but will stop at nothing to appropriate the land and property of blacks," Theodore "Ted" Edlich III of Total Action Against Poverty writes in a prepared statement that ran in Bishop's series. The effects of ill-considered decisions have been felt for decades. This grand mistake, Edlich writes, "has dampened the incentive of blacks to invest in their homes. It has created a sense of transiency which has been a deterrent to attracting business investment. It has created a sense of hopelessness and even bitterness which has been transmitted to a new generation of young people who have seen their parents exploited."

Urban Renewal: One Woman's View

Mary Bishop sums up the impact of urban renewal by sharing the vision of one elderly woman: "Pauline Stevens Kegler was born in the house her father built at 215 Patton Ave. N.W. She doesn't like to publicize her age; suffice it to say she has lived in that house almost every day of this [the 20th] century. The city came in and remodeled it for her a few years ago.

"From her front porch, she has seen some good years in Gainsboro. 'Everyone would get along all right together.' Neighbors visited each other. Sunday mornings, they'd all go off to Sunday school.

"'I knew all the people.' She doesn't now.

"Neighbors have moved away or died. The house next door hasn't been lived in for a dozen years. "'There's been 14 homes torn down on this block,' she says.

"She looks down the street at the rows of old houses set apart by empty lots as she says with certainty, 'After I'm gone, this will all be pushed down.'"

Urban Renewal throughout America

Roanoke is by no means the only American community for which, in hindsight, urban renewal efforts proved an unmitigated disaster. According to Fullilove, 992 American cities engaged in urban renewal. Though some failed to embrace it at the federal level, almost every city engaged in some homegrown version thereof by condemning individual homes or sections of neighborhoods for specific public-works projects such as highways, parks, or government buildings. The Roanoke documentation, says Fullilove, is "tremendously important because it's a small enough place that you can see the whole thing. It provides a case study of every American town and city." By contrast, the effects of urban renewal in New York City would be far harder to document because of the massive scope and scale.

Roanoke's tragedy echoes throughout America. In 2008, California's Bay Area raised the white flag on urban renewal efforts when the San Francisco Redevelopment Agency announced it was closing its Western Addition area office and campaign. The departure ended a 40-year urban renewal project "that was touted as a move to wipe out blight but actually destroyed the city's most prominent African-American neighborhood," according to the *San Francisco Chronicle*.

"Eminent domain was used to purchase Victorian homes and buy out local businesses" in the city's Fillmore District, writes *Chronicle* reporter Leslie Fulbright. "The thriving black business community" and the contiguous residential community were destroyed as owners were forced to shut their doors. Loans to black residents were almost impossible to come by. As a result, residents were forced to sell and move. Though promises were made to move people back to the neighborhood upon project completion, "the area sat empty for years," Fulbright writes.

Hard Numbers from the Western Addition Redevelopment Project

Timeline:

1948—Area declared blighted

1956—Demolition begins

1964—Area expanded to 60 blocks

Numbers:

883—Businesses closed
4,729—Households forced out
2,500—Victorian homes demolished
$50 million—Amount spent on the project

Courtesy of the *San Francisco Chronicle*

Rehousing America with What's Already Here

So what can be learned from the destruction of entire neighborhoods in Roanoke, Detroit, San Francisco, and elsewhere?

Lessons abound. A myriad of local cultures and ways of life have been swept away along with the buildings in acts of grave social injustice. As housing spirals toward board-up and teardown, communities become susceptible to the effects of crime, prostitution, drug use, fire, and fear. Property values plummet. Communities wither and go into decline.

One of the most significant lessons learned from the loss of inner-city neighborhoods is that the physical houses—no matter how seemingly flimsy, paltry, blighted, or outdated—constitute a valuable resource endowed with materials of real value, embodied energy, and significant history. These houses should never be dealt with lightly or paternalistically through "community betterment" initiatives that come from the top down.

While some in the preservation community actively engage in work to save teardown houses—that is, solid, habitable houses that may be stylistically dated or lacking in the latest bells and whistles—most groups continue to draw a distinction between this category of livable houses and foreclosed, blighted, and boarded-up inventory. *Moving toward the rescue of both categories of housing represents the next giant leap forward in rehousing America.* But for many Americans—incredibly, even those working in the affordable housing field—the reality of just how deplorable conditions are "on the street" is hard to fathom.

Stan Wilson's Directive: Considering the End Families in Need

Stan Wilson's life work focused on expanding and improving housing conditions for the less fortunate in Charlotte, North Carolina. Yet inside the confines of his comfortable offices in city hall, it was easy for the head of the city's Housing Department to become isolated from the realities faced by those in need. The group was large and growing. It included not only the homeless and displaced but those suffering from job loss, eviction, foreclosure, and substandard housing conditions. More and more white-collar workers who had lost their jobs or stretched themselves too thin (or both) were entering this unlucky camp every day.

Stan Wilson figured that his staff members—some 25 functionaries who spent their days in air-conditioned offices making decisions and writing reports—should lay their eyes on those in need of a roof over their heads—what he calls "the end families" they had been hired to serve. "At the city, we primarily provide funding to agencies and developers who go to work to build or rehab units for occupancy," says Wilson, who has since left that position to take a job as executive vice president of operations and planning for Builders of Hope.

For that needed dose of reality, Wilson elected to hold his agency's annual summer kickoff at the offices of Crisis Assistance Ministry (CAM), a local nonprofit offering emergency financial assistance for rent, utilities, and other critical needs. As staffers drove up to the CAM building that July morning in 2009, they received a visual snapshot that was nothing short of a wake-up call. People applying for assistance swarmed the building, making it nearly impossible to find parking. "The lots were jammed," Wilson recalls. "People had been waiting since five in the morning, trying to get rental subsidies. Outside the building was jammed, and so was the waiting room." The sheer *number* of people in need—women and children, entire families, the elderly, men in business suits—made a deep impression on Wilson's staff. After the official meeting ended, the group of ordinarily jaded government employees elected to volunteer for the ministry.

What Wilson's staff understood in the proverbial blink of an eye was a sobering reality little recognized in our nation today. America is in the midst of a housing crisis of enormous proportions—one that has hit not only home sellers, buyers, and lenders, who have received the lion's share of media attention on the topic, but also renters, roomers, landlords, and residents of every stripe.

Just as the housing bubble of the early to middle part of the opening decade of the new century fueled America's GDP, propping up housing prices, fueling new construction, and artificially boosting numerous other sectors of the economy, the Great Recession set into motion a downward spiral that squeezed people out of homes and reduced affordable housing inventory. It accelerated the existing trend of shutting down low-end housing; it jammed people into group homes; and it forced them to squat in vacant, condemned housing without plumbing or electricity. It lengthened already onerous waiting lists at homeless shelters and put all too many out in the street. At the same time, market conditions all but halted new housing construction at the lower end of the market.

Affordable Housing: A Dire Picture

Housing—at every price point and for every income level—is an essential barometer of the health and well-being of the nation. Until the issue is addressed and solutions identified, the crisis will continue, if not accelerate. Chris Estes, executive director of the North Carolina Housing Coalition, likens housing to "the hub of a wheel." The spokes that spring from that hub include transportation, health and welfare, homelessness, human safety, and school policy.

The latest report from the Census Bureau, released in September 2010, showed that one in seven Americans now lives in poverty, the highest percentage in half a century. Additionally, 2010 marked the third consecutive year in which the poverty rate grew. More than 14.3 percent of Americans—or 43.6 million people—live at or below the federal poverty level. The growing number has put pressure on all forms of assistance, public and private, including public housing facilities, homeless shelters, food banks, and poverty reduction programs.

Every demographic has been impacted in some way by the Great Recession. If anything good has come out of the downturn, it could well be a shift toward compassion and tolerance and away from stereotypes and misperceptions about those living in poverty housing. Because job loss, foreclosure, and displacement are close to almost everyone, those living in substandard housing are no longer "those people." The change is long overdue.

The overall affordable and low-income housing picture in America can best be described as dire—a crisis hitting those in need the hardest. More than 200,000 public-housing units have been lost since 1995, at a time when many authorities have converted their public-housing stock into tenant-based vouchers, according to the National Low Income Housing Coalition. For every 100 households with "extremely low incomes," only 37 rental units are affordable and available to them, said NLIHC board member Leonard Williams at a recent meeting.

Moving Forward with Hope VI

In the early 1990s, Henry Cisneros, then the secretary of housing and urban development in the Clinton administration, helped to create a government housing initiative called Hope VI. The program has pursued the admirable goal of creating mixed-income communities, rich with amenities, to address the isolating effects of monocultural and ghetto enclaves, thus providing a leg up to those in need. The program has spent $6.2 billion in federal money to demolish government housing, revitalize housing complexes, and plan for the future. Hope VI has allowed housing authorities to award displaced residents Section 8 vouchers—that is, coupons for private off-site housing.

While the concept accomplished many goals and has worked well, the on-the-ground reality is that enough money does not exist to fill the need. The net effect of Hope VI projects has been displacement for large numbers of dwellers in the neighborhoods where the projects have been constructed. The program has razed large swaths of public housing, effectively displacing thousands upon thousands of needy people.

"I feel that it [Hope VI] is destroying the health of America," says Mindy Thompson Fullilove. She likens this government housing initiative to a "new and improved" version of the failed urban renewal programs of the 1940s through the 1970s. Fullilove says that, despite the progressive rhetoric surrounding the program's goals, Hope VI in essence involves "pushing poor people out of the way so other people will have jobs. It's been hugely destructive to people and to cities."

Through a combination of factors including the Hope VI program, private market forces, and the overall economy, the number of existing affordable housing units has not only been declining, but new construction has virtually halted on low-income housing projects. This unfortunate development has occurred in the wake of the Great Recession. Two fundamental conditions are the driving forces. As of this writing in late 2010, bank financing for low-income housing is almost impossible to come by because the cost to build is greater than the appraised value of the properties when finished. Banks won't loan because no secondary markets want to buy the mortgages. The other crucial factor is that the motivation for most developers to build low-income properties—taking advantage of the available Low Income Home Tax Credits (LIHTC)—has all but disappeared with the erosion of black ink to write off.

Renters: Hidden Victims of the Foreclosure Crisis

Another factor contributing to the national shrinkage of low-income rental properties is the foreclosure crisis. While foreclosure tends to be understood as a phenomenon visited on owner-occupied properties, the reality is that approximately one-third of all foreclosures occur on renter-occupied homes, according to Kalima Rose, senior director of the Oakland, California–based PolicyLink Center for Infrastructure Equity. When landlords get into trouble, their tenants are likely to pay a high price, too. While many tenants in foreclosed properties are Section 8 renters (that is, those who receive federal housing assistance vouchers), others are moderate- and upper-income residents who live in upscale urban enclaves including single-family homes, condominiums, duplexes, and apartment complexes.

Providing some relief to unlucky renters is the Protecting Tenants at Foreclosure Act of 2009, a law signed in May 2009 by President Obama that requires leases to survive a foreclosure. In other words, tenants are allowed to remain until the expiration of the lease, while month-to-month tenants are given a 90-day eviction notice. Despite this new level of protection, many tenants find themselves displaced on short notice when their homes change hands. For instance, a tenant whose lease was near completion may have anticipated renewing but is suddenly shut out of that option and thus has to incur the financial, logistical, and emotional costs of relocation.

When mortgage holders (generally banks) become the new owners and seek to put properties up for sale as quickly as possible, renters can find themselves between the proverbial rock and a hard place. The servicing companies assigned by banks to handle these "properties in limbo" rarely consider the interests of outgoing tenants as a top priority. If the roof starts to leak or the plumbing goes south, it is the exception rather than the rule that the problem is taken care of expeditiously. "In many cases, tenants are still paying their rent," says Kalima Rose, "so those in default continue to get their money while the foreclosure proceedings are going forward." Unaware that the previous landlords are soon to lose the properties and have no interest in long-term maintenance, these tenants are almost never adequately cared for. If they do discover that the previous landlords have been foreclosed upon and direct their needs to the new landlords, they most often find no satisfaction there either.

Anecdotal evidence suggests a hardening of landlord response to tenant needs during the downturn. In today's economy, even landlords of income-producing properties may be cash-strapped. They use rental income to cover personal liabilities and are thus forced to defer maintenance.

Landlords may fail to fix things, and they may also fail to supply them. "In some apartments in Raleigh and environs, for instance," says Nancy Welsh, "the rule is you bring your own appliances. Can you imagine how difficult this is for a family who can barely scrape together the deposit on an apartment, let alone make the monthly rent and utility payments?" If the appliances are provided, the landlords may in some cases simply refuse to repair or replace them when they break.

Owner-occupied Foreclosures

Arguably the most heart-wrenching of all foreclosures are those in which people's long-term dwellings are lost or in which profiteers sell underqualified mortgagers a bill of goods, make off with their life savings, and put families out on the streets. Many of the people who have lost their homes were in properties they could not really afford in the first place. Often, these marginal and risky borrowers were practically handed the mortgages with no credit checks and zero down payments. Many were lured into home ownership by ARMs (adjustable rate mortgages) that delivered ridiculously low entry-level payments that ballooned as interest rates ticked upward. If it seemed too good to be true at the time the mortgages were rolling and the money was flowing, in fact it was. For many first-time buyers, those sweet mortgage deals went south as soon as house values started plummeting while their payments began skyrocketing.

In 2006, an estimated 1 percent of all United States homeowners went through the process of foreclosure, according to information provided by RealtyTimes.com. But by the year 2009, around 10 percent of Americans were at risk of foreclosure, according to the Mortgage Bankers Association. (Borrowers at risk of going south are red-flagged when they miss at least one mortgage payment.) Some of the potential foreclosures in 2009 were averted through negotiations with financial institutions to rework loans, or the properties were sold in advance of the foreclosures. Nonetheless, more than 900,000 homes were repossessed that year, according to data provided by RealtyTrac.com. That number was projected to increase by 100,000 to fully a million homes in foreclosure in 2010. By contrast, in the years leading up to the financial crisis, an estimated 100,000 homes were taken over annually by lenders.

The Stigma of Foreclosure

So how do these alarming numbers translate to the individuals affected on the ground? Once borrowers move through the system into foreclosure and lose their homes to banks or lending institutions, they are not only issued their walking papers but are also saddled with a nasty credit stigma that will haunt them for years to come. This black mark will adversely affect their ability to locate new places to live. Not only will they be excluded from buying for some time, but they frequently encounter enormous difficulties in finding places to rent.

During the economic crisis, many other borrowers have joined the ranks of those going underwater on their home loans. Job loss, the death of a spouse or parent, divorce, illness, or some other personal crisis may have prevented these folks from meeting their obligations.

The net effect of the foreclosure crisis has been an increased number of people who are either underhoused or out on the street. Once foreclosed upon or evicted from rental properties, many Americans turn to short-term housing fixes such as the charity of relatives and friends. Others make their homes in cars or garages or by squatting. Tent cities have sprung up in some parts of the country. Shockingly, people are even occupying crawlspaces in many communities. These "situationally homeless" people have joined the ranks of the chronically homeless. Their number is also growing, thus creating an ever-expanding pool of people without roofs over their heads.

Foreclosure's Impact on People of Color

While the ramifications of the mortgage meltdown have been far-flung, affecting every sector of American society, its effects have been most keenly felt by single mothers (and occasionally single fathers), people of color, and low-income families. The foreclosure crisis has dealt a harsh blow to traditionally African-American neighborhoods and low-income communities of color, impacting homeowners and renters alike. Sadly, as foreclosures multiply and prices for inner-city properties decline, these properties are often snatched up by investors and speculators who engage in a high-stakes game, using people's homes as pawns in the grand scheme of wealth building. Even if they start out with the intention of being honorable landlords, many investors rapidly morph into slumlords who view their properties as mere cash cows and care little about the livability, prosperity, and long-term sustainability of communities.

While slumlords who prey on poor inner-city residents with limited options are hardly new, worsening economic conditions have made the situation bleaker for those most vulnerable. Not only do tenants in low-income properties often suffer from inadequate landlord maintenance, but many face the pitfalls of eviction because of the challenging job market and increased financial pressures. It is not uncommon for families to live in fear of being thrown out, of being just one paycheck away from finding themselves out on the street, surrounded by their life's possessions.

The Search for Solutions

In light of this throng of displaced, homeless, and underhoused people, in light of a middle class that is financially stressed and challenged and that often cannot afford the houses that are on the market, what is America doing to respond? What solutions are being created? How is the nation going to house all of its citizens?

To their credit, housing industry professionals—including builders, developers, architects, lenders, municipal housing officials, and others—are scrambling to make sense of the need for housing, especially of the affordable variety. They are searching out new public-private partnerships and other innovative models. They are casting their eyes, maybe for the first time, on existing inventories of vacant housing stock, the price points of which span from the upper reaches to more modest levels. In their search for solutions, these professionals are taking into account the fact that it has become nearly impossible for many builders to act when the appraised value of completed homes can be lower than the cost of construction. Despite all the bleak news, creative solutions and striking new trends are emerging in this time of change and crisis.

Smaller House Size

Among the reduced number of houses that *are* being built today, average size has shrunk dramatically—and in a short period of time—demonstrating America's responsiveness to changing conditions. Boyce Thompson, editorial director of the *Builder* group of magazines, reported in September 2010 that the median size had registered what he calls "a steep drop, to 2,000 square feet, in the typical new home started during the second quarter of [2010].... The metric is down from about 2,250 in 2007." Thompson goes onto to debunk predictions that America will go back to building oversized "aspirational" homes once the economy recovers. "Buying a home today," he writes, "doesn't ensure future equity gains." In the near future, he predicts, buyers are likely to remain "more cautious and frugal."

"Responsive Housing Design": One Man's Solution

Ed Binkley is an example of an architect whose designs have undergone a profound metamorphosis. In the past, his focus was on designing upscale McMansions for clients with deep pockets. Indeed, he once created a concept home for golfer Tiger Woods. But the crisis of the last few years shook him to the quick and caused him to radically shift focus. Today, Binkley's interest lies in affordable green housing. He has created what he calls "the Shelter Series," which consists of high-density single-family houses ranging in size from 600 square feet to just over 900 square feet. These homes are situated on small lots; four units could fit onto a 70-by-120-foot parcel. The structures are inexpensive and can be built rapidly. He calls his new concept "responsive housing design."

"It's what anyone who's involved in affordable housing—and housing in general—should be focused on," says Binkley, who is based in Oviedo, Florida, near Orlando. In other words, housing should be responsive to the needs of clients, residents, and the community, along with the economy and the environment. Housing, Binkley says, should also be reflective of people's income levels. His goal is "dignified housing—not *just* housing."

Small Is Beautiful—Small Is the New Big

Binkley's vision for the housing of the future aligns with all current trends—including, of course, Builders of Hope's embrace of rescued homes of smaller square footage. In fact, he has drawn inspiration from such popular visionaries as Sarah Susanka, renowned architect and author of the *Not-So-Big House* book series. Another person of the same mindset is David Mauer, whose Raleigh firm, Maurer Architecture, specializes in adaptive reuse and urban restoration. Committed to preserving the historic aesthetic of existing buildings during restoration, Maurer Architecture created the façade design of Builders of Hope's State Street Villas community. Jay Shafer is another notable visionary. In 1997, Shafer, based in Boyes Hot Springs, California, created the Tumbleweed Tiny House collection, which features house plans with total square footages smaller than some people's closets. "My decision to inhabit just 89 square feet arose from some concerns I had about the impact a larger house would have on the environment, and because I do not want to maintain a lot of unused or unusable space," Shafer writes on his website. "My houses have met all of my domestic needs without demanding much in return."

Is Home Ownership Still the Dream?

The recent economic crisis has caused people to rethink and challenge many long-held assumptions. Near the top of that list is the concept that home ownership is a requisite of the good life. Sociologists and others are questioning whether or not home ownership should be a universal goal for working Americans. Thomas J. Sugrue, Kahn professor of history and sociology at the University of Pennsylvania, argued in a 2009 article in the *Wall Street Journal* that America needs to accept that home ownership is no longer a realistic goal for many and must curtail the enormous government programs subsidizing it.

At a grass-roots level, people are likewise challenging the idea that owning is a better bet than renting. Indeed, an article in the September 11, 2010, issue of *Time* magazine states that mortgages can be "a millstone" in today's economy. As workers change jobs and professions, "households are much more likely . . . to see income dip dramatically—even if only temporarily," the article concludes. "What families need in order to maintain income is the flexibility that home ownership works against."

Many Americans are waiting longer to buy new homes. With financing harder to obtain, larger down payments are required and stellar credit ratings and job histories are needed. Many people must sell their last home before they buy their next. That said, most Americans still dream of owning their own homes, as it represents solidity, stability, and the feeling of putting down roots. While the new economic landscape will continue to dictate how the issue evolves, it is safe to say that home ownership will endure and take on new and different forms.

Time for a New Paradigm

When a big-picture solution that works appears on the scene, old ways can collapse in a heartbeat. When people hear about the innovative model presented by Builders of Hope, the typical reaction tends to be one of disbelief. People use magical terms to describe it. "It's too good to be true," commented one housing professional upon first encountering the model. Iris June Vinegar, a Raleigh reporter who has published several articles about the organization, sent the following message electronically to Builders of Hope's director of communications upon learning that BOH would be featured on the *CBS Evening News*: "I knew from the moment I met her that Nancy was the best thing that ever happened to this city. Now I can say she's the best thing that happened to this country. She's also a P.R. dream. She rocks."

All hyperbole aside, part of what makes the Builders of Hope solution surprising is that it is so close at hand. The fact that a large existing inventory can be utilized—instead of destroyed—to jump-start a housing renaissance seems obvious. Why has this simple solution never been attempted on any grand scale before now?

Sometimes, the stars must align in order for a model or an organization to take off. That happened for Habitat for Humanity International after Jimmy Carter was defeated in his 1980 bid for a second term as president and came back to his home in Sumter County, Georgia. (Coincidentally, Millard and Linda Fuller had founded Habitat for Humanity in Carter's presidential year of 1976.) In short order, the former president accepted an appointment with one of the world's best salesmen and visionary leaders,

Millard Fuller. The rest, as they say, is history. Along with the charismatic Fullers, Jimmy and Rosalynn Carter helped to put the organization's name on the map and create a worldwide movement.

Rehab Is the Best Option

The time has arrived for Builders of Hope's rescue-and-rehab model, which is detailed in Chapter 3, to present itself full-blown to America. While house moving and green rehabilitation are not new, Builders of Hope is doing them in a way never before seen, with efficiencies of scale that deliver beautiful and energy-efficient homes. The model lowers the carbon footprints of residents by keeping energy bills low. It helps keep residents' finances sound by driving costs down to the range of affordability. It keeps construction materials and debris out of landfills and provides a valuable link to the past and to architectural heritage. It also broadcasts the message that *things* are important, too. It is better to take care of those things already possessed than to tear down and build new.

This model is not only restorative but also the greenest solution around. To date, new green construction methods have captured the lion's share of media attention. While they are significant, the preservation and upfitting of existing structures have to date been underrepresented in the nation's effort to create housing while simultaneously promoting sustainability and community. Now, in light of the economy and current depressed appraisal values, the real trick is how to make green building affordable. *Preserving the built environment represents the best solution.* Not only is tapping into existing housing resources the most affordable and available option, it makes the most sense from a conservation point of view. It preserves materials that are already in place and combats climate change.

Where to Go from Here: Reimagining the Future

Community life is a critical component of a healthy built environment—and one that has been lacking in so many American neighborhoods. Vibrant communities of the future—much like the dynamic pre–World War II African-American communities—will depend on deep levels of interconnectivity. Mindy Thompson Fullilove says that stability is a needed element of strong community life: "Generational knowledge is fundamental to health." Furthermore, neighborhoods need to be integrated into cities and regional systems that are equitable. "No neighborhood is an island. Being 'comfortable' in the midst of despair is a recipe for ill health," Fullilove says. "Germs and social disorder are no respecters of the artificial lines that impress people." What's more, she says that neighborhoods need to be "densely interconnected" and active so people are "bouncing off each other and generating the ideas that will sustain them in hard times."

The leadership of Builders of Hope has incorporated the creation of community into its model to rehouse America. It and other visionary organizations are reimagining the future of the nation's housing amid a landscape that is rapidly evolving. Americans cannot continue to do things the way they have always been done. Even if that were possible, the truth is that the system just isn't working anymore. We can no longer afford to tear down existing housing stock to make way for units that are by and large not as strong as the ones they replace. We cannot build houses that will last for only 20 years. We cannot continue to overlook or to discount the valuable resources embedded in existing homes.

What is on the horizon is revitalized, walkable, livable, sustainable communities built using existing inventory and arranged according to smaller-scale housing units, with an emphasis on affordable amenities, community centers, and outdoor interaction.

Not surprisingly, the revolutionary model presented by Builders of Hope has arisen at precisely the moment of crisis. While the embodied energy contained in older housing stock has always been there, never before has there been a greater urgency to save and use it. Never has the need been greater for the rapid turnaround that the Builders of Hope model demonstrates in renovating dilapidated and teardown housing and turning it into affordable residential space.

Stop tearing down and start building up! That is the message for the future. Builders of Hope is poised to lead the way to a fully housed America, a nation of greater justice and equality. What Builders of Hope presents is paradoxical. Its revolutionary model is at the same time startlingly obvious—using what is right under our noses as the basis for rehousing the nation.

Anti-teardown Preparedness Kit: Resources to Rally

- The National Trust for Historic Preservation offers wonderful resources for combating teardowns. Go to www.PreservationNation.org to read or download the following PDFs.
- Advocacy for Alternatives to Teardowns
  This step-by-step guide offers advice for mounting a successful campaign for alternatives and strategies for managing teardowns.
- Teardowns by State and Community
  The latest National Trust count of teardowns is broken out by states and communities.
- What's Wrong with Teardowns: A Visual Analysis
  Graphic illustrations help make the case for how teardowns impact older neighborhoods.
- Too Big, Boring, or Ugly: Planning and Design Tools to Combat Monotony, the Too-big House, and Teardowns
  This document offers planning and design tools to tame the too-big house, to shake free of monotonous development, and to negotiate the political minefield of teardowns. It is published by the American Planning Association.

The following websites may also prove of interest.

- http://www.westportnow.com/index.php?/v2/section/category/category/Teardowns/
  WestportNow.com tracks the progress of teardowns in a Connecticut community.
- http://www.preservemidtown.com/
  This is another sample website of a local organization—in Tulsa, Oklahoma, in this case—concerned with the epidemic of teardowns.

CHAPTER 3

THE BUILDERS OF HOPE MODEL: SUSTAINABLE REVITALIZATION

The core concept of sustainable revitalization is based on the principle of interconnectivity of communities and resources. Beginning with homes crying out for rescue, families looking for affordable, quality housing, and a work force in need of skill development and permanent employment, the Builders of Hope model is a practical and proven solution that addresses a myriad of economic, environmental, and social issues. The model was designed specifically for that subset of the population that falls between the cracks: the working poor and struggling middle class. In many urban areas, members of this group cannot find decent housing near where they work. Readers will learn how houses are identified, donated, moved, and rehabilitated and will gain insight about how energy efficiencies are embedded into each home. This chapter also examines how the economics work so that donors, buyers, renters, suppliers, employees, and communities all benefit.

A Revolutionary New Paradigm

Builders of Hope burst onto the scene back in 2006 with a startlingly simple idea, one that stood to revolutionize the world of affordable housing. The organization offered multipronged solutions to the cluster of issues surrounding urban blight and the deficit of affordable housing, as detailed in Chapter 2. Instead of demolishing outdated housing stock—according to the Environmental Protection Agency, an estimated 250,000 houses are torn down annually in the United States to make way for new development and construction—why not recycle, rehabilitate, and repurpose it as affordable housing? Amazingly, as obvious and straightforward as this approach may seem, no one had ever attempted it on any significant scale in America.

Enter Nancy Welsh, Builders of Hope visionary, creator, and founder. Once she—with the help of a trusted group of friends and advisors—was able to identify the moving parts behind the concept and put them all together into a workable, solutions-based process and package, the idea took off. The organization's model is built around the emerging principles of social entrepreneurship. Welsh understood early on that a traditional nonprofit funding model based solely on grants and donations would not—especially in the current economy—allow for the expansion of programs and markets at the rate needed to make substantive change. Internal sustainability—that is, financial self-sufficiency—was imperative for the organization to maximize its mission of transforming

America's inventory of teardown and blighted housing stock into affordable housing. To that end, BOH's financial model is based on multiple revenue streams: low-interest loans, partnerships with government agencies, revenue from rental properties and home sales, contracted services, and private sources (i.e., foundations, businesses, individuals, and faith-based and civic groups).

The Builders of Hope model sprang from identifying a large and growing gap between the need for and the availability of affordable urban housing solutions in the Raleigh, North Carolina, area. Infill and commercial redevelopment had effectively replaced a vast number of moderate-sized affordable homes with McMansions and upscale retail properties without replacing the lost inventory. The model addresses this need while introducing green building technologies to residences that the organization rehabs for low- and middle-income earners. Each project the organization tackles refines the process and at the same time expands its capacity to incorporate new technologies, materials, and methods into rehabilitated affordable housing. Collaborative partnerships with research institutions keep Builders of Hope on the cutting edge and give its homebuyers and renters the healthiest, most comfortable, and most affordable environments possible for building their lives.

The organization draws a distinction between *poverty* housing, in which inhabitants are unemployed or on government assistance, and *affordable* housing, the niche that Builders of Hope fulfills. Its brand of affordable green housing is primarily for middle- to lower-middle-income workers—police officers, teachers, nurses, secretaries, and service providers, those who have steady employment but for whom home ownership in safe neighborhoods is all too often out of reach.

Builders of Hope offers a "whole house" approach to saving and renovating individual homes in the context of creating new communities or restoring existing ones. By viewing the existing inventory of dilapidated and obsolete houses and buildings as an asset to be harvested rather than blight to be eradicated, Builders of Hope sets forth a revolutionary new paradigm that serves as a national solution for affordable housing creation.

National Demand for Affordable Housing

Because the nonprofit is uniquely qualified to meet the demand for green affordable housing with existing inventory, it is expanding rapidly from its home base in Raleigh. Phone calls and e-mails come into headquarters regularly from people wanting the organization to move into their communities.

And it's no wonder. When Nancy Welsh presents her model to audiences—young and old, socially disadvantaged and privileged, ideologically and politically liberal and conservative—she consistently receives a high level of enthusiasm and buy-in. "The overwhelming majority of times when we go in to make a presentation about our work," she says, "whether to bankers, funders, government officials, civic organizations, housing authorities, or regular church groups, people are blown away. They become emotional, even teary-eyed. It's as if people know in their bones that our approach is the right one. It just makes sense. It's good for the environment, the economy, and society. It's what you call a win-win-win."

The model resonates deeply with people on an emotional level. It brings forward the winning message that houses are not disposable items. Rescuing homes provides an invaluable lesson and an uplifting example to everyone involved. It says that no matter how low people fall, no matter what their struggles, they, too, are capable of rebirth.

"Nobody is doing anything like it [the work of Builders of Hope]. Very rarely does one get a double benefit, such as both economic and environmental advantages. And even more rarely, a triple when you add the social gain. It's really winning the trifecta for the whole community."

—Dallas developer Bennett Miller, who has been instrumental in establishing a Builders of Hope office in his city

---

Homeowner Association president Dawana Stanley and her family are proud of their new home at Barrington Village.

Three Primary Beams: Environmental, Economic, and Social

To borrow an analogy from the world of construction, Builders of Hope rests on three primary beams—*environmental*, *economic*, and *social*—each of which alone bears a heavy and significant load. The three beams offer multiple and overlapping benefits, each bolstering the other. For instance, the *environmental benefit* of salvaging homes improves the health of the planet, while "greenovating" homes by retrofitting them with environmentally friendly, state-of-the-art construction materials in turn positively impacts the families who live there.

The benefits of inhabiting eco-friendly homes are manifold, from lower utility bills (economic benefit) to better indoor air quality (health benefit) to the sense that residents are now stakeholders in reducing their carbon footprint and playing a role in the recovery of the planet (moral, social, and community benefits). The benefits make for healthier, happier, and more productive citizens—ones who become more generous and more fully vested members of their communities.

"I was overjoyed someone was thinking about the planet"

Dawanna Stanley bought a house with a yard at Barrington Village, Builders of Hope's flagship green community in southeast Raleigh, and moved with her husband and children from a rental unit in nearby Cary in 2008. She calls her new neighborhood "serene and peaceful" and has planted her first-ever garden there. The community is a far cry from the dicey New York City public housing project in which she grew up. First-time home ownership is a dream come true for the Stanleys. At 2,900 square feet, their house is larger than most in the development, but she finds it "just right" for their brood of five children. The fact that her home was recycled is a bonus. "I was overjoyed someone was thinking about the planet," she says.

In fact, environmental benefits stand as one of the "Big Three" in the Builders of Hope model. What is drawing national attention to the model is its innovative, integrative approach to the three key components of the organization's mission. This chapter will delve more deeply into each.

Environmental Benefits

"Remember, the greenest building is the one that's already built."

—Lew Schulman, president, Builders of Hope

Recycling Teardowns

From an environmental perspective, the Builders of Hope mission of saving homes is enormously important. Sparing homes from the wrecking ball and the landfill represents a major contribution to environmental protection and conservation. Nancy Welsh estimates that, as of this writing, the organization has saved more than 11 million pounds of debris from landfills. These savings are expressed as "vacated landfill space." As the organization grows and its model is rolled out in new communities around America, the savings have enormous implications. "The recycling of existing structures is essential to addressing waste now and in the future," says Lew Schulman, president of Builders of Hope. "Remember, the greenest building is the one that's already built."

The materials that went into the initial construction of rescued homes are saved when the houses are moved to new locations or rehabbed in place. These materials include timbers for floor joists, framing, and hardwood flooring. When such materials are allowed to carry on their useful life, additional trees don't have to be cut for new construction.

Of course, houses are not made from timber alone. Additional materials saved from rescue houses include everything from kitchen sinks to bathtubs to doors, from closet rods to shelving, from crown molding to door hinges to plantation blinds. In many cases, such amenities as granite countertops, tile, and hardwood flooring come with the homes. All of these components represent embodied energy and carry with them a carbon cost not only for their production but also for transport and installation. If the salvaged items have to be replaced with new ones, the carbon cost will obviously increase. Using things that already exist rather than replacing them minimizes the use of nonrenewable resources in the production of their new equivalents.

The big-picture benefit to the environment from rescuing and rehabilitating—*recycling,* if you will—teardown houses is tremendous. Taking a page out of the Bau-Biologie® philosophy, Builders of Hope adheres to the principle that what is good for the residents of a house is also beneficial for the larger ecosystem—the "earth home" all people share. To that end, making new homes as environmentally friendly as possible is a core component of the Builders of Hope mission.

Extreme Green Rehabilitation

All Builders of Hope developments follow the organization's proprietary "Extreme Green Rehabilitation" protocol. Each residential rehabilitation project presents unique issues that require distinct construction strategies for "greening" the home practically and affordably. The Extreme Green program was designed to identify and address these issues and to provide a roadmap for building crews to follow based on the condition of the homes and the intensity of the rehabilitation required. Developed with the support and expertise of Advanced Energy and the North Carolina Solar Center, the Extreme Green Rehabilitation program applies new green construction and energy-efficiency standards to rehabilitation projects.

Barrington Village opened in 2008 as Builders of Hope's debut community. One hundred percent of the "rescue homes" for this community in southeast Raleigh were physically relocated and placed on new foundations. To give the community continuity and a cohesive feel, each home was endowed with such architectural elements as a substantial columned porch and Shaker-style shingles. The Extreme Green Rehabilitation process was birthed at Barrington. "As innovators, we're always looking to push the envelope and improve the process," says Nancy Welsh.

Patent Pending: Protecting the Process for Affordable Housing

The rescue-and-rehab process developed over the course of greenovating the homes at Barrington Village is now the model for the signature Extreme Green Rehabilitation protocol. The organization currently has a patent pending for its methods of creating affordable green communities, according to Dennis L. Boothe Jr., general counsel for Builders of Hope. "We sought this patent in order to keep our unique green building methods in the affordable housing arena," he says. "We are interested in producing consistent housing product, and a livable and sustainable home environment for work-force families across the country. The patent allows us to maintain control over how our process is replicated."

The Process at Work

The Extreme Green Rehabilitation process starts with donated structures. Homes that would otherwise be torn down to make room for new construction or as a result of other development pressures are offered to Builders of Hope. Prospective donations are inspected for structural integrity and such issues as termite damage and untreatable rot. The houses are also evaluated for usability, desirability, and movability. (Occasionally, homes in mint condition are offered up, but due to their difficult locations, timeline problems, or other logistical issues, they cannot be accepted.) People often assume that blighted and boarded-up buildings are beyond reclamation. "But when we hear of a home slated for demolition or are offered buildings in a sad state, we're never discouraged. We go out to take a look," Welsh says. "People are amazed at what we can take. What treasures we find hidden in the blight!"

On average, around four out of five homes that are evaluated meet the organization's standards, says John Jenkins, head of house moving for Builders of Hope. Even vacant and boarded-up properties are often in better shape structurally than they may appear from the curb.

Upon acceptance, the houses are either scheduled for relocation or assigned to Builders of Hope's "rehab-in-place" program. Before houses are moved, exterior brick and any bump-outs such as porches, additions, decks, and garages are removed. Sometimes, all or part of the roof is removed. In addition, any asbestos abatement work is done prior to transporting the houses. Lead-based paint is removed from donated homes by a state-certified firm or certified employee after the homes have been moved and before

The house mover transports a rescued home to State Street Village in downtown Raleigh.

any work is done on them. All homes are tested and are required to be lead-safe when work is complete.

Before a house is moved, new concrete footings are poured and allowed to set up. The home is then moved over the footings, leveled, aligned, and stabilized on cribbing so the wheels can be removed. Next, the foundation wall is built, leaving holes at the lower end for the steel to be pulled out from under the house after it is placed on the new foundation. The Builders of Hope team then strips each house down to its studs, removing plumbing, wiring, and the original HVAC ductwork. On occasion when time permits, this stripping work is done prior to the move. The house is then readied for its transformation.

Customized Home Design: Co-Creators of Their Living Space

One of the most unusual and noteworthy aspects of the Builders of Hope process is that in most cases the houses are presold before the green rehabilitation takes place. This strategy offers advantages to both the organization and the buyers. The first advantage is financial. Money doesn't have to be spent on "spec homes." In most cases, the homes aren't transformed until buyers actually commit to the purchases and the bank loans have been preapproved.

From a buyer's point of view, what could be better than having a hand in the creation of one's own home? Unlike so much affordable housing—which is delivered with cookie-cutter floor plans and bland design elements—the Builders of Hope model allows its clients to behave like pricey upscale buyers. Clients become, in effect, co-creators of their living space. Nancy Welsh relishes putting what she calls "the power of choice" directly into buyers' hands.

Here's how the Builders of Hope design process works. After the lot is selected, the sales agent helps the buyer identify which of the homes is right for her, taking into consideration house size, sales price, utility bill projections, and more. For a development like State Street Village in Raleigh, for example, Builders of Hope designers created recommended floor plans and elevations for houses slated for donation that had not yet been moved. Those homes were offered to potential buyers in a kind of matchmaking process.

After reviewing the preliminary floor plan, the potential buyer may tour the hull of the home. At that point, the home has likely been stripped to its studs (with salvaged items set aside for reuse) and is ready for transformation. "In most cases, the house doesn't look like much at this stage," observes Welsh. That is one reason why having floor plans and renderings of the home's exterior is so important. With those instruments, she says, "buyers can visualize their future home."

Though the level of deconstruction varies with each home, a buyer—working in conjunction with Builders of Hope's in-house architect—can often make changes to the layout. Once the potential buyer has settled on which home works best, she meets with sales and design staff to discuss her specific needs and desires. For instance, a single mother with a teenage son may choose to turn a three-bedroom, one-bath house into a two-bedroom, two-bath. A home for an elderly couple may be made handicapped-accessible. For a single person, an extra bedroom might be made into a giant walk-in closet and bath suite. This process allows awkward or unnecessary walls to be removed to open the flow inside the house.

As much as possible, the design is created with sensitivity to existing materials, especially in houses with hardwood flooring and high-quality cabinetry. Maintaining existing resources saves money while enhancing the beauty of the homes. Upgrade options include kitchen islands, stainless-steel appliance packages, and customized blinds, which can be prehung if customers so desire. While the options vary from one BOH community to the next, buyers are free to select exterior siding colors from a preapproved palette.

Eco-Friendly Materials and Energy Efficiencies

Once the plans have been finalized, the next phase is the total rebuilding or "greenovation" of the house. When new materials are to be incorporated into the renovation, care is taken to select environmentally friendly choices and to employ waste-minimizing construction techniques. Workers retrofit each home with a modern HVAC system, along with new plumbing, wiring, and siding. Low-emissivity (low-E) double-pane Energy Star® windows are installed except in communities where historic covenants apply.

A new roof comprised of standard asphalt shingles, generally in a light color to reflect the sun, is laid. (However, for rehab-in-place, retaining such historical elements as old tin roofing may become an architectural priority.) The crawlspace is sealed, and the underside of the floors is sprayed with foam insulation. This high-performance insulation sets the stage for interior comfort and reduced utility bills.

"We're really creating a brand-new structure out of preexisting framing and interiors," says Lew Schulman. "The homes are rehabbed to the point you can call them 'new' for insurance purposes." Practically speaking, each of the rehabbed homes qualifies for a new "effective built date" in the year in which the Extreme Green Rehabilitation is completed. Despite the complete greenovation, fully 65 percent of the original structure remains on average.

What Does *Green* Mean? A Statement from Nancy Welsh

At Builders of Hope, *green* means we make old new again. And at Builders of Hope, *new* means healthy, sustainable, and affordable—affordable to live in and affordable to maintain. We believe the resources already exist to build housing that is affordable and healthy, that revitalizes neighborhoods and creates economic security for hardworking families and their communities.

We've created a model—Extreme Green Rehabilitation—that captures our philosophy and goals, and it has set a new industry standard. The process guides rehabilitation through home assessment, site selection, relocation, construction debris management, and reconstruction with green building practices, materials, and landscaping.

Among the key green features of the protocol are

- The recycling of existing homes and usable materials

- The development of in-fill locations when possible
- Sustainable building practices and materials
- Passive solar orientation
- High-performance, closed-cell spray-foam insulation
- Exterior ventilation
- Low-E windows
- Low-flow plumbing fixtures
- Energy Star® appliances and water heaters
- Low-VOC materials and sealants
- Compact fluorescent lighting
- Sealed envelopes, including sealed crawlspaces with insulation
- Large front porches to reduce heating and cooling bills
- Rain barrels and drought-tolerant landscaping

We at Builders of Hope are committed to building the healthiest, most energy-efficient, and most affordable homes possible for the individuals and families we serve. Therefore, our construction team stays abreast of the rapid improvements in the green building industry and adds those improvements to our process when they're proven. To ensure that all families living in Builders of Hope homes receive the maximum benefit from green components, we also offer an educational program about their homes' features and maintenance.

Reducing Construction Waste

One of the ways Builders of Hope continuously reduces its construction waste stream is by striving to reuse the materials indigenous to the house. When elements torn out of a house are not needed, they're stored off-site at a BOH warehouse for future use. Whatever is unsalvageable is recycled or discarded. Items saved from one home—such as textured paneling from a den or the hardwood flooring from a second story removed when the house was converted into a one-story—are used in another.

Whenever she sees material that can be put to use, Welsh challenges the crew to get creative. "I remember seeing some leftover framing wood, and I asked the guys to put in some built-in bunk beds and window storage boxes."

As the organization evolves, its goal is to bring down waste to almost nothing. "I want to get to the point where we can reuse or recycle 99 percent of what comes in," Welsh says, acknowledging that this is a lofty goal. Already, she is sketching plans for a reclamation resale business that would give away such items or sell them at nominal cost to low-income families that are rehabbing houses in Builders of Hope revitalization areas and corridors.

Get Outside: Creating Community and Green Landscaping

Builders of Hope's eco-friendly mission does not stop at the house's perimeter but extends into the out-of-doors. Water-conserving rain barrels are standard issue on all BOH homes. These garbage-can-sized receptacles are connected to gutter downspouts, enabling residents to harvest rainwater off their roofs as an alternate source for yard and garden needs, which is especially important during dry spells. Drought-tolerant and native shrubbery, trees, and grasses are used for landscaping. Recycled brick chips serve as water-permeable parking surfaces in some communities.

Slow-growing, drought-tolerant Bermuda sod is rolled onto the yards. "Does it make sense to spend extra money on Bermuda sod?" John Jenkins asks. "Absolutely! It is easier to establish than conventional seeded lawns." This, he points out, is especially helpful for first-time homebuyers, who may not have experience caring for lawns. What's more, Bermuda sod requires minimal watering and will withstand heat.

Porches are included on all the houses in order to promote relations among the new residents. These connections—neighbors looking out for neighbors—are essential building blocks of community life. A part of Builders of Hope's mission is to create communities. The organization promotes getting people—especially children—outside, in nature, to relax, exercise, garden, and play.

A Barrington Village house being moved

Barrington Village: The Work Begins

As Builders of Hope's first planned community, Barrington Village was a remarkable beginning, the place where the model took shape. Nancy Keates, a writer for the *Wall Street Journal*, opined in an article published in the fall of 2008 that Barrington might just be "the most politically correct housing development on the planet." Without a doubt, it remains a model of residential adaptive reuse most noteworthy for the originality of concept and execution.

Not content to rest on its laurels, however, the parent organization is still growing the model and improving and expanding upon its impressive debut community. "The model continues to evolve through a dynamic interaction with our partners," says Nancy Welsh. "Nobody has figured it all out yet, including us. We want to stay on the cutting edge, pushing the envelope on being green and keeping it affordable."

Ground was broken at Barrington Village in the fall of 2007. The organization employed wise land stewardship practices by clustering 24 homes onto a 7.8-acre parcel. "The typical house that we move is a ranch-style home with the long side facing the street," says John Jenkins. Lots in most new communities today are 40 to 50 feet wide and 100 feet deep. Generally, the houses have to be pivoted so as to present themselves in shotgun style. For instance, a ranch house may be rotated from a horizontal presentation to a vertical one. "The front door is moved from the

On both of these houses, new sheathing was installed on the ends where garages used to be attached. Those ends have now become front entrances.

long side of the house around to the end of the house," explains Jenkins. Often, other changes are called for as well.

Some of the homes at Barrington were positioned to capture passive solar effects, and they were all outfitted with generous front porches for efficiencies in heating and cooling. Organization leaders developed strategic partnerships with Advanced Energy and the North Carolina Solar Center to pursue the goal of making every house energy efficient with superior indoor air quality.

In BOH's next green community, State Street Village—developed in partnership with the city of Raleigh—each of the 25 homes is a green gem. In fact, 20 of them are registered to qualify for LEED (Leadership in Energy and Environmental Design) certification, as are all of the neighboring rental villas. To save on utility bills and create a more comfortable indoor environment, care was taken to seal all building envelopes. Energy Star® appliances and light fixtures using energy-saving compact fluorescent lighting come standard on all BOH homes. The homes were also outfitted with low-flow faucets and commodes, which provide long-term water-conservation efficiencies.

Green Rehab Helps Address Health Issues and Indoor Air Quality

While reducing utility bills and lowering carbon footprint remain primary goals for the rehabs, another strong imperative driving the use of eco-friendly and nontoxic materials is bolstering the health of the residents. It is estimated that most people spend as much as 90 percent of their time indoors, where, according to the Environmental Protection Agency, levels of air pollutants may be up to five times higher than outdoors. Unfortunately, much of the nation's affordable housing stock is built with inexpensive materials and minimal concern for their impact on indoor air quality.

Generally speaking, the worst offenders are the lead dust found in older homes containing lead-based paints; glues and formaldehyde in cheap cabinetry, countertops, closet doors, and vinyl flooring that give off volatile organic compounds (VOCs); and carpeting that traps allergens and gives off gases containing chemical components. Glues and matting that hold carpet in place are also responsible for giving off noxious fumes. Poor ventilation systems that circulate toxic substances—often sending biological irritants such as mold and mildew through filthy ductwork into the air—also contribute to degraded indoor air quality. These conditions create an environment that increases the risk of such respiratory diseases as asthma. Many such issues can be alleviated by upgrading to healthy materials and employing building practices that reduce health risks to vulnerable populations.

The next stage: adding front porches

Cohesive architectural elements create a uniform look for this neighborhood of rescued homes from all over the city.

Children at Risk

Children (along with the elderly and those with chronic lung disease, cardiovascular disease, and diabetes) are among the most vulnerable to poor indoor air quality, according to a 2004 report issued by the American Academy of Pediatrics Committee on Environmental Health. Babies, children, and even teenagers are more affected by air pollution than adults because their respiratory defenses are not fully formed. Their smaller airways are more likely to become blocked when irritated. Because children breathe more rapidly than adults, they take in more polluted air per pound of body weight than do grownups.

Nancy Welsh was struck by a presentation made by Rebecca Morley, executive director of the National Center for Healthy Housing. Morley presented evidence that increased asthma rates are tied directly to gasses from inferior building materials and poor indoor-outdoor air exchange. "She related that children who grow up in lower-income housing have exponentially higher rates of asthma than those who grow up in market-rate housing," says Welsh. This correlates with more doctor visits and missed days of school. Welsh says she resolved on the spot that "every Builders of Hope home would be built to deliver superior indoor air quality."

One of the goals of Builders of Hope is to provide all housing units—both homes for sale and rehabbed rental units—with systems that improve indoor air quality for residents. Whenever possible, BOH communities include amenities such as ceiling fans to improve air circulation and flooring made of tile and solid wood, which is easier to clean and less likely than carpet to hold and release toxic residues. Taken together, these and other measures contribute to healthy indoor air.

Energy Efficiency Makes Affordable Housing Sustainable

Rising energy costs and shrinking wages have forced lower-income Americans to spend a greater proportion of their income on utility bills. "The affordable-housing population is most vulnerable to rising utility costs," says Krista Egger, director of Affordable Housing for Advanced Energy in Raleigh. "The less they spend on utilities, the more they can spend on health care, food, and other necessities." According to the United States Department of Housing and Urban Development, the cost of utilities imposes "a disproportionate burden on the poor." For example, for those living on Social Security, the average energy burden amounts to 19 percent of income. For those receiving Aid to Families with Dependent Children, the energy burden is "seven times greater than for families at median income," with an average of 26 percent of income going toward energy costs, according to HUD data. This compares to an average of less than 4 percent of income going to energy bills for families earning median income.

To help make Builders of Hope homes affordable for residents over the long haul, the organization incorporates strict energy efficiency criteria into its green rehab model. All of its homes, including rentals, offer a guarantee that the energy used for heating and cooling will not exceed a specified amount for a period of two years after the rehabilitation. For example, as of this writing, an average 1,100-square-foot home in the Raleigh area would be guaranteed at $45 a month. If the bill is higher, a third-party certifier covers the cost overrun, along with the cost of identifying and remediating any problems behind the overrun.

All of these green building principles, taken together, contribute to a significant positive environmental impact in both the short and long term. They also impact the overall health and well-being of the planet.

Life-Cycle Assessment for a Builders of Hope Home

A recent study by two North Carolina State University graduate students, "Life Cycle Assessment of a Specific Residential Home: A Builders of Hope Case Study," offers significant corroborative data concerning the reduction of harmful environmental impact. The study, authored by Steven Pines and Tyler Strayhorn, compares the environmental impact of a conventional stick-built home with that of a Builders of Hope "move-then-rehab" home. The reduction of greenhouse gas emissions was significant with the latter. An average-sized Builders of Hope home—a 1,187-square-foot structure on Lot 15 at State Street Village—was used for the study. The BOH method of construction for the home offset 19.36 tons of carbon dioxide, or CO_2 Equivalence. The CO_2 Equivalence produced from the Builders of Hope model was nearly 50 percent lower than for the new-construction model. Expanded across the neighborhood of 25 homes at State Street Village, that would amount to roughly 484 tons of CO_2 Equivalence.

These impressive findings deal only with the construction process up to the completion of the house. If one takes into account the future carbon savings due to high energy-efficiency standards over the home's entire life cycle, the greenhouse gas offset is even greater. Additionally, the numbers do not take into account the amount of resources diverted from the landfill, according to Landon M. Lovelace, BOH's director of planning and sustainability.

Economic Benefits

More immediately tangible to the residents of Builders of Hope communities and other rehabbed homes is the inherent—and immediate—economic impact of sustainable homes: lower heating, air conditioning, and water bills. All of these factors directly affect the investment of finances and time that owners must make in their homes. According to the Builders of Hope philosophy, *affordability* means more than the sale price or monthly rental of a completed rehabilitation. An affordable home must remain manageable to the resident long after the closing or move-in date.

The Four-Dimensional Timetable

Driving down costs and accelerating project completion is one of the most unusual—and advantageous—components of the Builders of Hope model. What is the factor that allows the nonprofit organization to achieve these goals? The fact that all of the key players in the rehab process are in-house is the organization's greatest "secret weapon."

"We are the owner, the general contactor, the architect, and the builder," says Nancy Welsh. This allows Builders of Hope to run on its own accelerated timetable with green-lighted projects. Further, it allows the organization to respond quickly to changing market conditions.

"When you're talking about real-time direct input from various players, this approach provides cost and time efficiencies," Welsh says. "Instead of us going to the architect to ask him or her to come up with a floor plan, then going to the general contractor and asking if he can retrofit it, once we decide to do something, we can cut through months of frustrating delay and move quickly." Since all these key players are on the same team, the major work can be done in a session or two. "Everyone's at the table who needs to be at the table," she says, "discussing floor plan, rehab, greening, and work flow. If there's a problem in one area that impacts another, it can be addressed then." The team is flexible and resilient enough that if delays are presented at one work site, for instance, an immediate decision can be made to put that project on hold and to move to the next project on the list.

Because the homes are donated, soon-to-be "new" houses begin their rebirth embedded with significant equity. The organization benefits from economies of scale, from its ability to acquire some key elements in the homes at cost or for free, and from trained work crews that are well versed in the ins and outs of rehab.

Because of its partnership orientation, the organization receives gifts in kind from a variety of companies to further reduce rehab costs. For example, the General Shale Company of Raleigh has donated brick for all of the projects in the region. Builders of Hope receives inventory such as 12-inch tile, double vanities, and programmable ceiling fans from big-box home-improvement stores. Such enhancements contribute to the value and quality of the homes without pumping up the price tag. The market-rate amenities Builders of Hope is able to provide without increasing the cost turn the homes into highly sought-after commodities, even in the current depressed economy.

The Economics of Home Donation

Builders of Hope relies upon home donation as the basis for its economic model. Early on, when the BOH concept was just taking shape in Nancy Welsh's mind, she did the math and figured out the value inherent in the shells of stripped-down homes. She also realized that people owned homes that they might wish to donate for any number of reasons.

Here's how the home-donation process works. Say a donor has a house that he wants to tear down. Perhaps this donor has decided to build a larger "dream home" in its place. Maybe real estate in the area has grown more valuable than the house occupying it. Maybe the teardown house is on the "hit list" because of development pressures. A university may be expanding, or a freeway or a shopping center may be coming in, putting the house on the path to peril. Numerous reasons exist for why perfectly decent houses are torn down in America today. Whatever the motivating force, if an individual homeowner or developer plans to tear down a home, he may have to pay as much as $15,000 or more for demolition, abatement, and hauling away the debris to the landfill.

Builders of Hope offers an attractive alternative to those with teardown houses on their hands. If the nonprofit organization accepts the structure, the donor may be able to write off a significant percentage of its value on his personal income tax return. To simplify the donation process, the organization has developed a paint-by-numbers approach that sets out for people the sequential steps they must take in order to donate homes. BOH assists them in securing the necessary permits and transfers of ownership and connects donors with reputable service providers who offer the requisite asbestos testing and abatement, if needed. Once the houses are relocated to new sites, contractors certified in lead removal address any lead issues, following EPA guidelines.

Sometimes, municipalities further sweeten the pot for potential donors. For example, the city of Durham, North Carolina, has made the option attractive to potential donors of vacant, blighted housing by offering to forgive nuisance liens on the properties in exchange for their donation to Builders of Hope or other nonprofits.

In the organization's infancy, its principals had to go out and sell the model to potential donors in order to increase awareness of the benefits of the concept. They identified individuals and organizations—such as local governments, school districts, and even commercial and large-scale residential developers—that might be interested in donating one or more houses.

Back in 2006 and 2007, teardowns had reached epidemic proportions in Raleigh. Between 30 and 50 houses were being torn down every month, according to Welsh. "I used to keep my eyes peeled for candidates. You're driving down the road and you see a For Sale sign on a little ranch house that has two office buildings next to it," she says. "You know it's only a matter of time before it's coming down." She and her team were successful in those early years in convincing property owners to donate.

One of the most effective marketing strategies was pretty basic. Welsh had the idea for a yard sign reading, "Why Demolish? Donate!" The signs went in front of rescue homes before and after their moves. Likewise, houses being moved were sheathed in banners carrying the same attention-grabbing message.

Over the years, as Builders of Hope has gained prominence in the Triangle and garnered high-profile media coverage and

"Why Demolish? Donate!" signs are placed in front of donated homes during the deconstruction and house-move prep stages.

endorsements from city, county, and state government officials, word of mouth about the organization and its work has grown. Now, calls about houses come in on their own. "There have been a number of occasions when we've had more houses than we could accept," says John Jenkins, director of house moving. "But whenever we can, we try to check them out and, if they're good ones—really good, solid homes—store them for future use." However, to spare expense, Builders of Hope prefers not to move the same house twice.

With only a few memorable exceptions, most would-be donors have sparked to the idea that donating their properties was good for the bottom line, good for families seeking affordable housing, and good for mother earth. The folks at Builders of Hope call this the "triple green bottom line."

Homes Sold at Cost Deliver Built-in Equity

One of Builders of Hope's primary goals is to provide affordable housing that will enable owners to build equity, thus contributing to their long-term financial well-being. "Traditionally, home ownership has led to wealth creation," says Nancy Welsh, "and ultimately stability in our society." Instead of trying to pump up the organization's revenue stream, management made the strategic decision at the outset to pass along the captured revenue in its model to buyers—the people Builders of Hope was created to serve.

The jaw-dropping reality is that, to make the homes affordable, *they are sold at cost.* The finished houses are sold *below* their true market (or replacement) value. Even in the economic downturn, the following base prices for Builders of Hope houses on the Raleigh market in 2010 are impressively low. (Final prices can go up or down, depending on customization choices and upgrades.) For instance, in the State Street Village green community development just minutes from downtown, the Kampala, a three-bedroom, two-bath home at 1,187 square feet, sold for $135,000. The Cranbrook, another three-bedroom, two-bath home at 1,104 square feet, went for $127,000. The West, a 1,050-square-foot, two-bedroom, 1.5-bath house, carried a price tag of $124,500.

House pricing is structured to incentivize investment and long-term ownership. Restrictions based on HUD requirements tied to specific grants call for a minimum of 70 percent of those buying into these communities to earn 80 percent or less of area median income (AMI) and to be first-time homebuyers. The remaining 30 percent of the housing stock can be sold at market rates and with no restrictions to those making AMI or above.

For targeted buyers whose incomes are at 80 percent or less of AMI, certain restrictions apply. In order to qualify for the houses at below-market rates, buyers must sign what is called a "recapture agreement," meaning that if they sell the houses before 10 years have elapsed and make a windfall profit, they must repay a certain percentage. "This proviso is designed to prevent people from coming in and buying up the houses for low prices and flipping them," Welsh says. It also ensures the "longevity of affordability" that community planners are so eager to incorporate. An added bonus is that buyers are happy to know their houses are worth more than what they are paying for them. "One of our buyers at State Street who's been in his house three months told me he had the house appraised, and it was valued at $25,000 more than he paid," Welsh says. "It gives them a sense that they're building toward the future."

Habitat for Humanity provides its own mortgages. But prospective BOH homebuyers have to meet normal bank-loan criteria for conventional, FHA, and other financing. Buyers must hold steady employment over a 12-month period and show respectable FICO scores and debt-to-income ratios. Because of the houses' built-in energy efficiencies, some bankers dealing in Energy Efficient Mortgages (EEMs)—a HUD product—factor in lower

Example A. Before: the Barmettler.

Example A. After: the Barmettler. *(Photo by Jennifer Kromhout)*

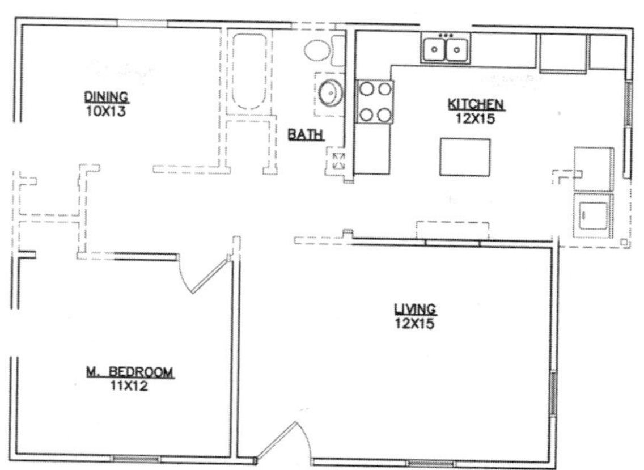

Example A. Before floor plan: the Barmettler.

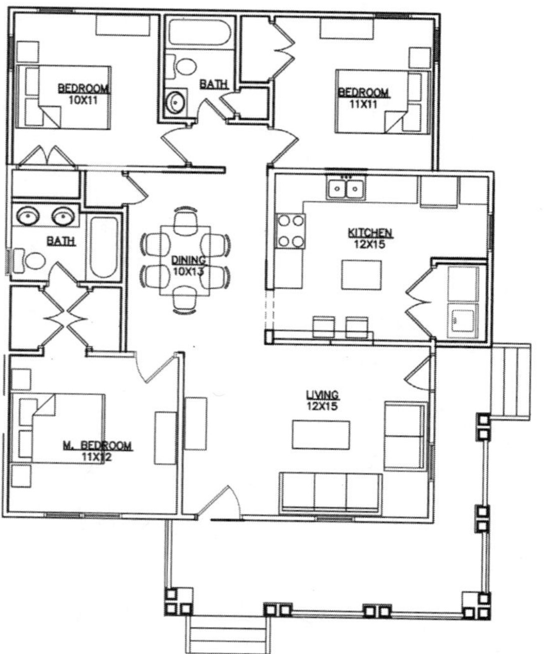

Example A. After floor plan: the Barmettler.

Example B. Before: the Evans.

Example B. After: the Evans.

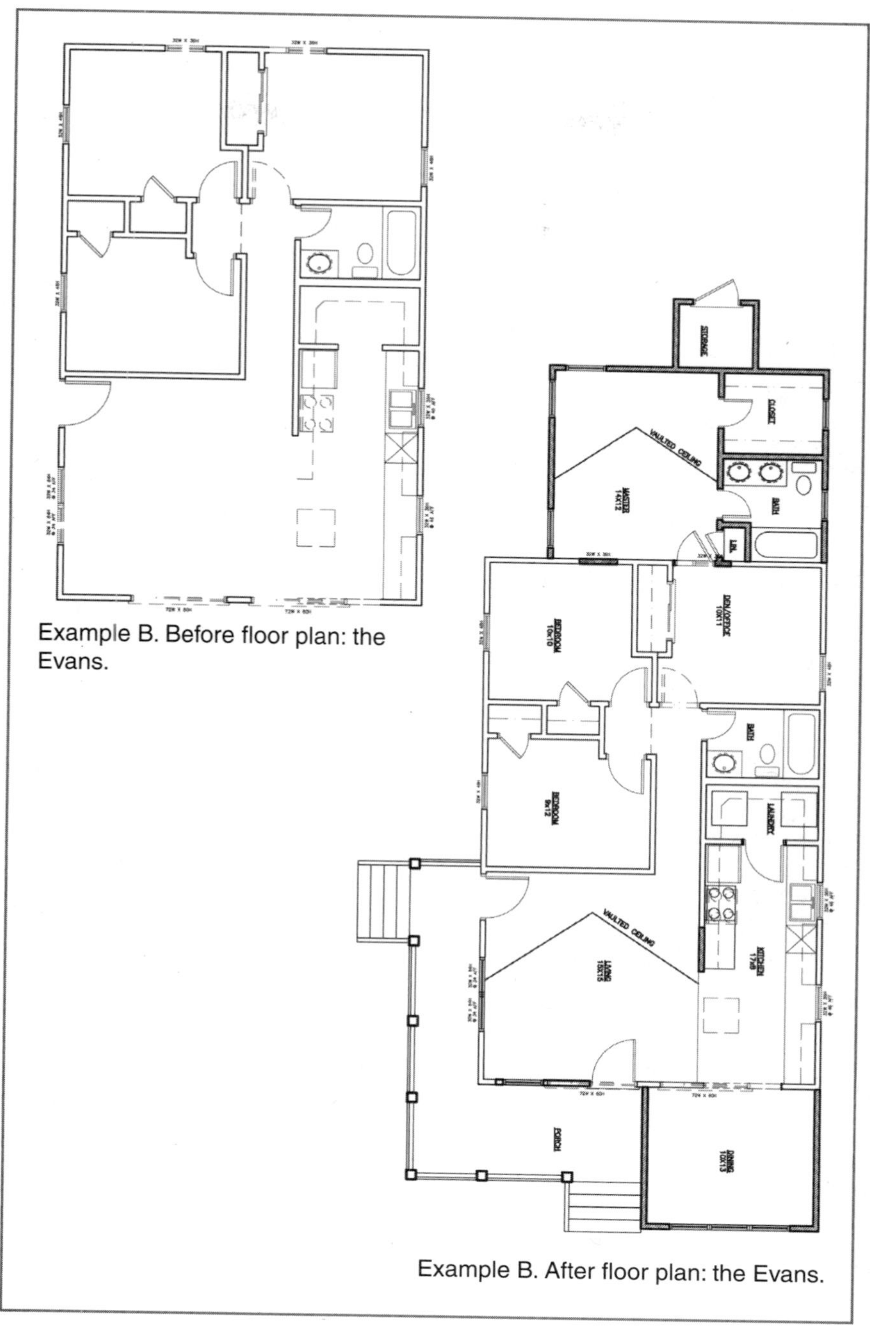

Example B. Before floor plan: the Evans.

Example B. After floor plan: the Evans.

Example C. Before: Green Level.

Example C. After: Green Level.

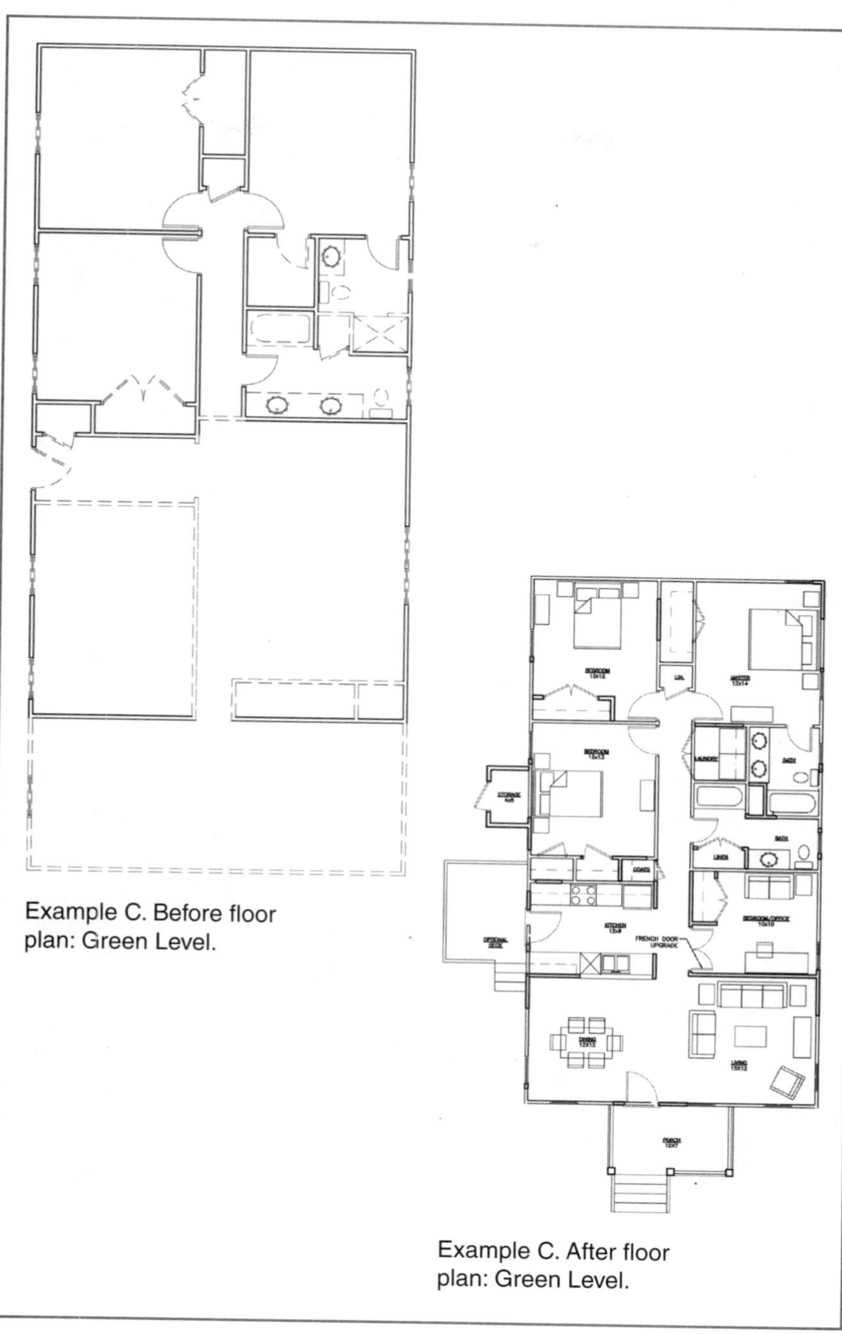

Example C. Before floor plan: Green Level.

Example C. After floor plan: Green Level.

Example D. Before: Green Level 2.

Example D. After: Green Level 2.

Example D. Before floor plan: Green Level 2.

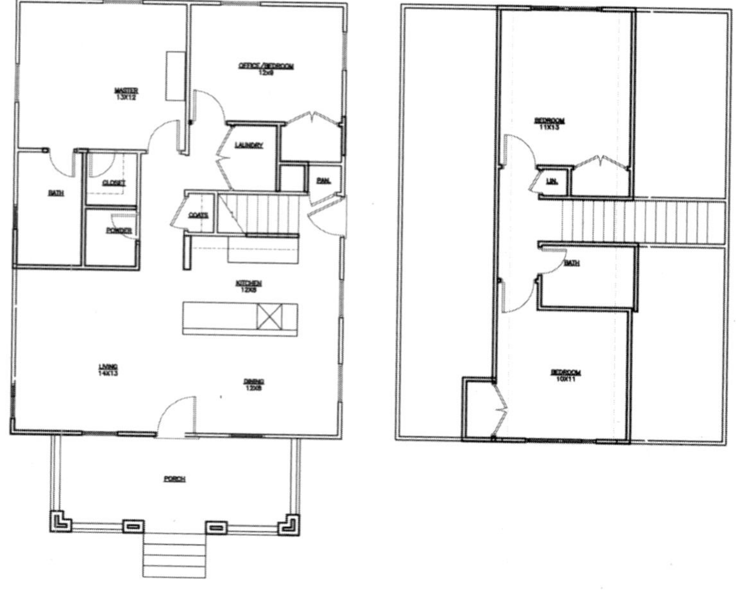

Example D. After floor plan: Green Level 2.

utility bills when developing their cash-flow projections. At State Street Village, for instance, the System Vision certification program guarantees heating and cooling bills in most homes not to exceed $45 monthly, versus more typical bills of over $100.

The economic impact of energy-efficient homes—from lower utility and water bills to the benefits of low-maintenance, drought-resistant landscaping—directly and favorably affects the bottom line for homeowners. What this means is that homes are economically sustainable in the long term, well after the closing date.

Lease-with-Option-to-Purchase Program

Qualifying for a conventional loan is a stretch for some potential buyers. Those falling into this category may make enough money but have poor credit histories, or they may have underreported past income on their taxes and need to properly report their income for a year. To help this clientele get back on track, the organization has developed a "lease-with-option-to-purchase" program to enable individuals or couples who are working to put their finances in order to get a Builders of Hope home. The organization generally doesn't approve any applicants for lease-with-option-to-purchase who wouldn't qualify for a conventional loan in a year's time.

Builders of Hope compels lease-with-option-to-purchase candidates to meet quarterly with a homebuyer counselor to be sure they stay on course, says Welsh. "The beauty of the lease program is that we can put future buyers in their homes right away. Once they move in, just being there, along with regular counseling, motivates them to stay on the financial straight and narrow in order to be able to purchase the home." Though the lease-with-option program is not yet a widely used instrument for BOH home sales, leaders project that it will become more popular in the future.

A Focus on Affordable Rental

In order to maintain property values in its green EcoLogical Communities, Builders of Hope requires that all homes be owner-occupied, with no rental options available. A covenant to the effect that buyers cannot purchase homes and subsequently rent them out is written into the purchase agreements.

That said, the Builders of Hope principals are well aware that the demand for quality rental properties at affordable price points is greater than ever. In fact, about one-third of all American households currently live in rental units, and the need is growing while the supply of available homes is dwindling. "Since 1993, the stock of low-cost rental homes has fallen by more than 1.2 million," according to material published by the John D. and Catherine T. MacArthur Foundation. "And more than one million are at risk in the decade ahead. At the same time, various forces, including demographic change and mounting foreclosures, will likely increase the number of renters by two million."

Builders of Hope has jumped in to help fill the gap. The organization has expanded its rental division, brought on dynamic new leadership to head it up, and is hard at work devising new, multipronged solutions and strategies to meet the growing need. It is now partnering with nonprofit and for-profit entities alike to rehabilitate former slumlord properties into affordable green units.

Drawing on the same cost-cutting, value-adding principles that guide the development of its for-sale Green Hope Community homes, Builders of Hope is tackling larger rehab projects such as State Street Villas, located close to its residential ownership community, State Street Village. At the same time, the organization continues to acquire homes in revitalization areas along transit areas to greenovate under its rehab-in-place program.

An example of a neighborhood that Builders of Hope has begun to transform is Lyons Park–West End in Durham, a city that has over 4,000 board-ups, largely due to the deteriorated tobacco industry. This historically African-American neighborhood, once characterized by strong community life, had hit rock bottom in recent years, falling victim to the effect of drugs, crime, and urban blight. In 2009, Builders of Hope acquired nine homes along Rosedale Avenue and transformed them into affordable rental properties, bringing a marked improvement to the area. Once the neighborhood begins its ascent with upgraded rental housing stock and enhanced community life, people will buy with greater confidence. "That's the long-term goal," says David Welsh, vice president of property management and Nancy Welsh's younger brother. "The immediate goal, however, is to provide safe, healthy housing for the population in the neighborhood."

"A new beginning": One Man's Story

Charles Joyner, 75, moved into one of Builders of Hope's newly greenovated one-bedroom duplexes on Rosedale Avenue in Durham in August 2009. The move represented what he calls "a new beginning" in life. Joyner grew up in the West End, close to his current residence, and remembers a happy though structured life as an athletic, enterprising youth in the 1930s and 1940s. Growing up surrounded by friends, relatives, and watchful neighbors, he was free to wander the neighborhood to play but never stepped too far out of line. "If you were not behaving properly, the news would get home before you did." He was six years old when Pearl Harbor was attacked. His mother was dressing for church, he recalls. "I ran up and down the street knocking on doors, telling everyone, 'We're all going to war!'"

Charles Joyner has made a satisfying return to his old neighborhood. (Photo by Blake Rothwell)

Growing up, Joyner developed his natural vocal talent by singing in the streets of his neighborhood and performing in the First Calvary Baptist Church choir. After receiving a bachelor's degree in political science from North Carolina Central University in 1957 and serving in the military for two years in Korea, he traveled the world as a professional singer. His career—which encompassed stage, radio, and television—took him to England, Scotland, France, Germany, Denmark, Italy, Canada, Korea, Mexico, and all over the United States. Joyner performed as a tenor for the Deep River Boys and also sang backup for Harry Belafonte and Brook Benton. In 1962, the Deep River Boys cut an album in Denmark. Today, Joyner pulls from a drawer in his new home a magazine layout in which he and his fellow band members were photographed in the company of a bevy of beautiful Danish models.

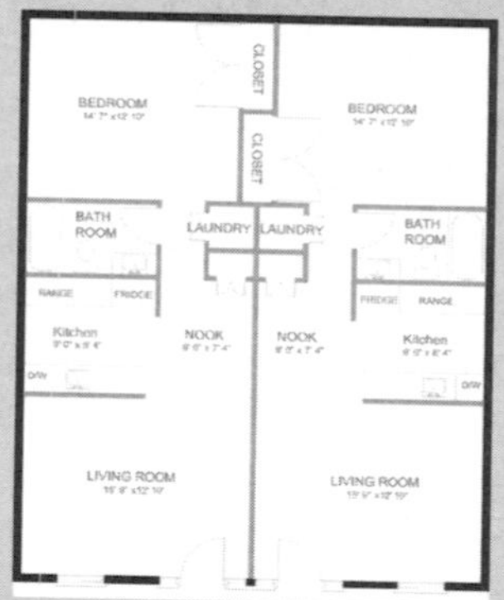

Example E. Rosedale Avenue duplex floor plan: Rehab-in-place.

In 1968, Joyner returned to Durham, where he focused on local venues, performing with the NCCU Drama Department and directing bands in area hotels and supper clubs. He suffered an enormous emotional setback when his only daughter was killed at the age of five in New York City when she was hit by a car.

In the late 1960s, the West End was already in decline. But in recent years, the area had fallen to the point that it bore no resemblance to the neighborhood of Joyner's youth. "It was down," he says. "Anything in life—even areas—can reach a bottom point. This street had become the pits. It was so different from what it was when I grew up. It was drug-infested, dangerous." Joyner says he has tremendous admiration for what Builders of Hope is doing to regenerate the area he has always loved.

For five years prior to moving into his Builders of Hope duplex, Joyner lived two streets over in a substandard rental unit that was dreadful in every way. The plumbing was faulty, and so was the wiring. "You were afraid you'd start a fire whenever you cooked because you'd blow out a fuse. It was depressing to

Example E. Before: Rosedale Avenue.

walk into a kitchen where you almost felt contaminated trying to wash dishes in your sink." The sink was constantly stopping up, with grease and grime flowing in from the neighboring duplex. "I got tired of buying Drano," Joyner says. "I'd call the landlord, and he would send a plumber, and it would work for maybe three or four weeks before the problem came right back. In the meantime, the week after the plumber was there, the landlord sent me a bill for $220. I refused to pay it. From that time on, he kept adding that $220 onto my rent."

Example E. After: Rosedale Avenue.

Joyner now pays $425 a month for his Builders of Hope apartment. His heating and air-conditioning bills are guaranteed not to exceed $25 a month. He credits the new place with improving his life immeasurably, taking him, as he puts it, from "night to day." He's sleeping much better and eating better "because there's less stress." Comfortable with his new home, he is happy and proud to have friends and family over. "We sit and watch a ballgame or listen to music." His new goal in life is "to enjoy every day." It's a goal he appears to be reaching.

Example E. Closeup: Rosedale Avenue.

National Affordable Rental Crisis: Not a Pretty Picture

Having a safe, affordable, and healthy place to live sets the stage for a good life, as in Charles Joyner's case. His success story is one of many that Builders of Hope employees relish. Matching tenants like Joyner with affordable new homes is one of the organization's primary missions.

The organization has made a point of studying rental rates at affordable housing communities around the nation. Builders of Hope's David Welsh says that what emerges is not a pretty picture. "It's disheartening to see what some organizations charge for rent." Nancy Welsh picks up the thread: "There is one self-identified affordable housing community that's always patting itself on the back for what they're doing for low-income occupants. But their cheapest rent is over $800 a month for a two-bedroom apartment. In New Orleans, you can't get a decent two-bedroom for less than $900." Welsh argues that what others are calling "affordable" is based on the cost of comparable units, rather than on what people are able to pay. "You can't say your $825 is 'affordable' just because the unit next door goes for $1,125," she says. "Affordability is only relative to the amount of money your demographic has in their pocket to spend. You can't price affordable housing off of comparables. You need to do your research and find out what people can afford to spend for housing in that particular community."

The mission of Builders of Hope is to provide affordable green housing to as many clients as possible. To that end, management has made a strategic decision—and a commitment—to keep rents low, rather than trying to maximize its rental revenue stream. It bases its rents on renovation costs for the property, not market conditions. If the organization needs $600 a month to cover the costs of renovation and overhead, $600 is what it charges, though the market might bear $900. "We're not out there to capture as much as we can but to make it as affordable as possible," says Welsh. "Our model aims to serve the community and meet its specific needs. It comes down to that."

Finding affordable rentals for people who would prefer to buy has certainly been one of those specific needs during the recent financial crisis. Those who have gone through foreclosure must establish good credit and endure a waiting period before applying for home loans. The organization had the foresight to move into rentals when the residential housing market collapsed. "We're solutions-driven," says President Lew Schulman. "When the economy changed, the demand for rental skyrocketed. Builders of Hope expanded its model to include truly affordable green rental."

Cutting the Cost of Transportation

With its State Street Village and State Street Villas communities in Raleigh, Builders of Hope delivered yet another benefit for its residents: transportation savings. Providing buyers and renters with close-to-town housing gave residents the option of utilizing public transportation. If they owned vehicles and commuted, living close to their work reduced transportation costs, including fuel, maintenance, and wear and tear on their vehicles. This also freed up precious time for family and community.

The Community Benefits, Too

From a big-picture perspective, the community at large reaps economic benefits from the work of Builders of Hope. The organization revitalizes neighborhoods by turning abandoned properties back into vibrant, safe, and occupied housing. Local governments profit when Builders of Hope rebuilds neighborhoods and thus increases the tax base. This in turn helps pump revenue back into municipal infrastructure and services.

Builders of Hope's two major programs—its EcoLogical Communities model and its rehab-in-place protocol—offer economic benefits for communities. The scourge of vacant and abandoned properties is a long-term problem for most major metropolitan areas. An abandoned property, according to *Blight Free Philadelphia*, a study published in 2001 by Research for Democracy, dramatically reduces the value of nearby properties. According to the report, houses 150 feet or less from a vacant building experienced a net loss of value of $7,627, a number that has likely increased in the decade since the report was published. What's more, the existence of vacant and blighted properties increases the cost of city services through greater numbers of crimes and fires.

"We cannot rebuild America by tearing it down first. From a national perspective, the damage to the environment and community from tearing down far outweighs any economic advantage."

—Nancy Welsh

The sad reality is that the vacant, aging property inventory is growing in most cities throughout America. The situation is epidemic, and teardown has been the prevailing response. This trend has been exacerbated by growing foreclosure rates. This makes the Builders of Hope solution more compelling than ever.

How the Model Works

Builders of Hope's first community, Barrington Village, was well under way before the economic crisis hit. Here's how the model worked. The organization purchased the land on which the development was to be located, paying cash. That asset was then leveraged for a development line of credit with the bank. Once the roads and infrastructure were in place, the organization began moving in houses and beginning rehabilitation. Once the houses were set on their new foundations, Builders of Hope pulled a 75 percent loan-to-value equity line on them to pay for the rehabilitations. As the houses were rehabbed and sold, the organization began to pay down the development line, so it was fully paid before the neighborhood was sold out.

Because Builders of Hope was still in its organizational infancy when the housing market went south, Welsh, Schulman, and other members of the brain trust had to think on their feet and work fast to develop new strategies and identify opportunities to enable the model to adapt and survive. As a result, Builders of Hope has had to form creative partnerships to continue providing affordable housing solutions.

Green-Collar Job Creation

Job creation is one of the most fundamental goals of the Builders of Hope model. The organization creates "green-collar" jobs in a challenging economy, while at the same time providing workforce training and temporary work for a new demographic. "We're creating *local* green jobs," says Welsh. "We're taking people and putting them back to work." In addition to its own crew, Builders of Hope commits to hiring local licensed subcontractors for each new project in which they are needed, thus providing employment to community residents and stimulating the local economy. As the organization replicates this model in other cities, it will continue to create jobs that can never be exported offshore.

Social Benefits

HopeWorks Program

Central to the Builders of Hope mission is its innovative work-mentor program, HopeWorks, which is at heart a green jobs training program for those with barriers to employment. Program participants include the homeless, at-risk youth, and ex-offenders. Once these people sign onto the program, they're given a six-month mentoring program during which they are trained in eco-friendly rehabilitation construction skills. In addition, mentees learn such primary workplace competencies as professionalism, courtesy, and respect—tools they will need to maintain permanent employment. During the course of the work-mentor program, they are paid hourly wages while gaining financial-responsibility skills through partnering agencies.

This construction training program gives participants the skills and experience to qualify for mainstream work and the life-skills training to maintain workplace positions. Establishing and expanding partnerships with the social-service organizations that supply the program participants make a positive impact on the local work force and economy and provide tangible social benefits to the entire community.

Community Creation: Building Social Infrastructure

The core Builders of Hope model, Building Green Communities, creates an enclave of security for working families in the form of cul-de-sac communities. This third key component of BOH's primary mission entails working in partnership with other organizations that have complementary expertise to create a comprehensive community stabilization plan. In addition to building physical infrastructure in the form of rehabilitated housing, BOH seeks to *create social infrastructure* via resource sharing and community building. The establishment of a homeowners' association is an integral component of the organization's EcoLogical Communities.

Nancy Welsh believes that BOH's middle-class to lower-middle-class clients should be given a greater array of housing choices than high-rise towers and poor-quality townhouses. Yet in the creation of new affordable housing these days, the focus is almost exclusively on multifamily complexes, she says. By contrast, the Builders of Hope model offers the American dream of single-family homes at affordable price points. "Just because you're earning below median income, does that mean you shouldn't be able to live in a single-family house anymore? Does that mean your kids don't want or need to play outside in the backyard, or that you shouldn't be able to have cookouts on your deck in the summertime?"

Preservation Sets the Tone for Community Building

Rehabilitation of older housing stock—the architectural DNA of a community—preserves the atmosphere of older single-family neighborhoods and promotes historical accountability, community, and stability. Preservation and rehabilitation set the proactive tone for the Builders of Hope model. Bringing old structures back to life puts everyone from the work crew to neighbors to future residents in a positive frame of mind for the holistic community-building work to come. The Builders of Hope construction crew and subcontractors are well versed in the sensitive nature of reconstructing older homes and take great care to preserve the character of buildings. "These older homes are treated with the respect they deserve," says Darryl Colwell, BOH's vice president of construction services. "They're like older people not sent out to pasture but given a place at the head of the table."

Creating a Cohesive Streetscape

The Builders of Hope design team works to promote community connection through the smart arrangement and orientation of houses and the incorporation of uniform design elements. At State Street Village, for instance, it created a cohesive streetscape by means of generous front porches with substantial columns perched on brick pedestals, cement-board siding, and a clustered orientation with matching elevations to connect the houses one to another. The orientation also cleverly masked size disparities among the homes. "When you enter the cul-de-sac," commented a first-time visitor, "you feel a sense of cohesiveness, of belonging, even though the houses were originally built miles apart and come from many different decades."

The model continues to evolve. The design of State Street Village brought the Barrington look to a new level. Barrington's vinyl siding was upgraded to State Street's premium fiber-cement siding, which features a historic color palette, resists cracking, and provides a more upscale look and feel.

The Power of Porches

Porches are the metaphorical bridges to the walkable, livable, sustainable communities that Builders of Hope is in the business of creating. They are a central component of all BOH houses. When building a community, the idea is to get people outdoors, connecting to each other. "You want to pull people into the front yard, as opposed to pushing them into the backyard," says Nancy Welsh. When people visit outside, they make greater connections to each other, generating an enhanced sense of physical safety.

"When you know your neighbor and his family members and feel connected to that family, you're more likely to invite him over for your Fourth of July cookout, and you're more likely to keep an eye on his home and alert the police if something doesn't look right," she says. This is how neighbors are made. This is how safety nets are woven.

In an ideal universe, Welsh would prefer commodious front porches. In the words of Vermont-based landscape designer Julie Moir Messervy, porches are "a room outside." But sometimes financial constraints make compromise inevitable, as was the case at State Street. Indeed, because the city of Raleigh required that the porches at State Street Village be made from poured concrete rather than the less expensive pressure-treated lumber used at Barrington Village, the porches were necessarily downsized, though they remained large enough to accommodate active front-porch life.

"On a lot of today's new marketplace houses, you've got a tiny little front door and all this garage," Welsh says. Society shows its treasure by giving cars front-and-center placement and casting aside community spaces like front porches. "At Builders of Hope, we prefer to put our money into conditioned living space," she says. "With limited budgets, our buyers would rather have a 1,200-square-foot house than a 900-square-foot house with a 400-square-foot garage." To accommodate vehicles, Builders of Hope plans call for concrete driveways along the sides of houses. The driveways provide enough space to park one and sometimes two vehicles. Sidewalks lead to the homes' generous front porches.

Community Gardens

To combat the "nature-deficit disorder" prevalent in contemporary American culture, as diagnosed by author Richard Louv in his book, *Last Child in the Woods*, Builders of Hope planners work to incorporate such outdoor features as community gardens and walking paths into new communities. At State Street Village, one of the homebuyers has already volunteered to spearhead a community garden project in a designated space adjacent to his property. This veteran gardener has offered to mentor others in the community and teach gardening skills.

In the future, Builders of Hope plans will include community gardens to promote vegetable, flower, and container gardening among its residents. Beauty and pride in ownership go a long way toward creating safe and stable neighborhoods. In the future, "we'd love to incorporate and encourage such ideas as water features, focal points, and walkways," Welsh says. "Quite simply, we want to encourage people to congregate outside. Spending time together in the great outdoors builds bridges in a way that little else can."

Bridging the Technological Divide

Internet access is another social benefit that Builders of Hope delivers as often as it can. In its EcoLogical Communities, for instance, the organization engineers and installs (in partnership with One Economy) wireless Internet access for all residents. The design team at the nonprofit understands that the Internet access that middle- and upper-class Americans take for granted needs to be available to help BOH residents step up or stay in the game. Being able to tap basic resources such as medical advice and to fill out job applications and complete student homework online has become increasingly important. It costs those who don't have access time, money, and opportunity.

Nancy Welsh points to a single mother with two young children who moved into Barrington Village, where she received a donated computer and Internet access. The enterprising young householder—who by day worked at a call center—immediately signed up for online MBA courses, which she took at home. Without the Internet connection, she never would have been able to work toward the degree. Getting out of the house for night classes was simply not an option.

Builders of Hope continues to develop the environmental, economic, and social components of its model. It may discard certain elements and incorporate new ones. "With each project, we improve the process while expanding our capacity to incorporate new technologies and materials into homes affordably," says Emily Egge, BOH vice president. Each city the organization enters presents new opportunities, partners, and challenges that further refine the model. As market conditions change, opportunities present themselves, advances are made, and responsible financing mechanisms develop.

Builders of Hope continues to stay on the cutting edge, giving its homebuyers and tenants the most comfortable and affordable environments in which to build their lives. Yet the core concept of sustainable revitalization based on the principle of the interconnectivity of communities and resources remains. It begins with homes crying out for rescue, families seeking permanent housing, and a work force in need of skill development and permanent employment. The specifics of the programs and protocols will evolve, but the fundamentals will never change.

CHAPTER 4

HOPEWORKS: BUILDING WORK FORCE AND COMMUNITY

One of the most visible and transformational components of the Builders of Hope model is its signature HopeWorks work-mentor program, in which those with barriers to employment—the homeless, ex-offenders, and troubled youth—are offered the chance to gain on-the-job skills in the field of green rehabilitation. This pioneering program is an integral part of each project the organization tackles. HopeWorks—which seeks to rehabilitate lives along with structures—addresses the social component of Builders of Hope's three-tiered model.

"Saving a house is a wonderful thing, but how can it compare to saving a life? If you can do both at the same time, you are working miracles."

—Nancy Welsh

Green-Collar Training for the Chronically Unemployed

When Builders of Hope was founded back in 2006, Nancy Welsh developed a model for creating affordable housing by rehabilitating teardown properties for the working poor and the struggling middle class. The "rescue houses" themselves were probably the single most significant component of the Builders of Hope model. But Welsh set her sights on doing more than just recycling houses. She wanted to rehabilitate lives. To that end, she created HopeWorks, a pioneering work-mentor program to address the social component of her three-tiered model.

HopeWorks is at heart a green jobs training program for the chronically unemployed. Individuals with barriers to employment—such as ex-offenders, the homeless, and at-risk youth—are taken through a six-month job- and life-mentoring program in which they are trained in "green-collar" construction skills and given hands-on guidance in the basic but crucial workplace competencies they will need to maintain permanent employment.

A Cornerstone of the BOH Model

"Some of the very first workers we used for our debut project at Barrington Village were work-mentees," says Welsh. While the program continues to be improved and refined, it has consistently served as the conscience of the organization, a kind of company cornerstone that inspires employees, funders, residents, and other stakeholders. "Saving a house is a wonderful thing, but how can it compare to saving a life?" she says. "If you can do both at the same time, you are working miracles."

As of this writing, numerous HopeWorks program graduates have moved on to the Builders of Hope full-time employment roster. Several others who completed the program but whom the organization couldn't hire have found steady jobs with BOH partners, vendors, and subcontractors or elsewhere in the construction industry. "We do everything we can to help them find work," says Darryl L. Colwell, vice president of construction services. "But even if they don't have jobs when they graduate, they have a skill. After the skill, the next most important thing they obtain from us is a *recommendation*—someone to vouch for their reliability and effectiveness." What's more, each graduate receives a certification of completion, which carries significant weight in the workplace.

For those who have benefited from the program, it quite literally represents a new lease on life. "Nancy took a chance on me," says Douglas Farror, 46, a Builders of Hope full-time employee who got his start in March 2008 through the work-mentor program. "I have not let her down." Farror performs a variety of tasks including demolition work (his favorite) and removing wire, scrap metal, and miscellaneous debris from beneath teardown houses before rehab-in-place begins or after the houses have been moved to their new lots. He recently joined a team of BOH staffers traveling to New Orleans to participate in a major volunteer event.

Farror's success story is one that quickens the hearts of Builders of Hope's mission-driven employees. Almost everyone who works for the organization shares the sentiments of their leader in their desire to make the world a better place. A pragmatic idealist, Nancy Welsh established the HopeWorks program so her organization could be "part of the solution," she says. Though her own life experience has largely been one of material privilege and comfort (see Chapter 1 for more on Welsh's story), she has always identified with those less fortunate than herself, with people who have more obstacles than options.

People Who "Deserve a Second Chance"

Of the three categories of workers in training on which Builders of Hope focuses its efforts, ex-offenders are the most numerous.

Though the road to employment is challenging for the homeless as well as for at-risk youth, ex-offenders arguably have it worse than those in the other groups. "This is a population that is discriminated against for housing and employment for the rest of their lives, due to the fact that they have an ex-offender banner hanging over them that will never be erased," says Welsh. "Ex-offenders, just like the rest of us, are men and women who need to be forgiven and deserve a second chance." In North Carolina alone, 25,000 prisoners are released into society every year. Three-quarters of these parolees are nonviolent offenders who have served five years or less. Many of them, according to Welsh, have sound job skills, but their biggest hurdle to getting their lives back on track is finding anyone willing to hire them.

Barring any outside help, the reality parolees face is discrimination at every turn. When they fill out job applications, they are inevitably asked if they've ever been convicted. This question puts them in a tough position. If they tell the truth and check "Yes," they are invariably blackballed from jobs. If they lie and check "No," they are subject to automatic expulsion should their falsehood ever be discovered. These difficult circumstances are exacerbated in an ailing economy, when the job market is flooded with applicants.

"Holding offenders for their crimes and then releasing them into a society that will not house them or employ them perpetuates the cycle of illegal activity," says Welsh, who draws inspiration from Gandhi's famous quote, "Be the change you want to see in the world," which is framed and prominently displayed in the Builders of Hope foyer. "They may want a new life, but they're forced back to lives of crime for lack of other options, just to survive."

Welsh goes on to say that society has established "a caste system similar to that of India," in which a certain class of people, in this case ex-offenders, has little or no opportunity to cross back into normal society. Like India's untouchables, America's ex-offenders are relegated to slum housing and unemployment. "These are people that society has literally thrown away," concurs Alex Henzel, Builders of Hope's social programs manager. Through its Hope-Works program, BOH seeks to remove barriers to employment for a group of ex-offenders and welcome them back into society's fold.

Profile of a HopeWorks Participant

"I'm not proud of my past, but I'm proud of my future."

—Sam Jones

Weekday mornings, Sam Jones is up by five o'clock to start his day with Bible study and devotional. After a full day at his construction job, during which he helps renovate buildings for affordable housing, he returns to the in-house facility, a part of Hoskins Park Ministry's outreach program, where he lives with other men whose pasts have brought them together to form an unlikely household. Jones's evenings are filled with more study and the fellowship of others who, like him, have been homeless and served time in prison. These days, Jones takes deliberate, minute-by-minute steps to stay sober, to stay employed, and to surround himself with faith. He is surviving, but not in the same way he formerly viewed survival.

Jones's story is hardly unique; the hard circumstances of his youth are shared by many. On his own since age 14, he ended up going from one situation to the next but primarily living on the streets. School became irrelevant; finding food and protection from the elements were his goals every day. He drifted into substance abuse and then found that selling drugs provided a livelihood that fit well with his own increasing dependence. Prison was inevitable.

"I'm not going to do this anymore"

Upon his release from prison, Jones discovered that no one would hire him. The job skills he had managed to acquire along the way didn't matter. In one telling experience, he lied about his criminal background to get hired into an entry-level position at a car-care facility. He worked there nearly a year and did such a good job that he was promoted to manager. At that point, the company ran a formal background check, found out he was an ex-offender, and immediately fired him. "Everybody shot me down," he says.

Old acquaintances—drug dealers who offered him a place to live until he could find a job—resurfaced. Of course, they knew the chances of an ex-inmate finding employment were virtually nil, which was just what they were betting on. After a while, they told Sam he needed to start paying for the food he was eating and the new clothes he was wearing; they told him he needed to get out there and begin selling again. He looked at his future and asked himself if, at age 40, that was all his life was going to amount to. "Enough of this," he said. "I'm not going to do this anymore." Sam Jones put on his old clothes—the ones he had worn out of prison—and walked away. He was done with that life.

The Difference between Then and Now

With that one step of faith, doors started opening. After finding his way to Hoskins Park Ministry, Jones began putting his life in order. But employment continued to be just out of reach. That's when Builders of Hope entered the picture. It was something unique—an employer that didn't just *consider* hiring those coming out of prison but specifically *sought them out.* It represented the answer to a lifetime of disappointments. When a friend wished him luck on the way to his interview, Jones replied that he knew in his heart the job was already his, that the appointment was "just something to get dressed up for."

Life didn't suddenly become free of challenges for Sam Jones. Although some days are tougher than others, he no longer feels alone, and his work with Builders of Hope is a big part of re-creating his life. There is little doubt that Jones possesses the qualities and the determination to achieve the future he envisions for himself, which includes perfecting his carpentry skills, helping others like himself find their way to a better life, and one day having a home of his own where his two teenage sons can be with him and witness firsthand the power a man has to change. "I'm not proud of my past," he says, "but I'm proud of my future." It is a future filled with pride. Builders of Hope is based on the belief that, just like the buildings rescued and restored, every human being has the right to a new day.

Rehabbing Homes, Rehabbing Lives

The metaphoric link between rehabilitating lives and houses is not lost on Nancy Welsh. Nor is it lost on the workers in training. "They come in and look at these houses and see that the houses need to change from the inside out, just like they do," she says. "It's not unusual for workers to say things like, 'When I came here, I was all torn down, just like this house. Through my work, through rebuilding my life, I've become whole again.'" Accounts of troubled souls being reborn after immersing themselves in such therapeutic and rejuvenating pursuits as gardening, farming, and art are legend. The common denominator is engagement in new creation.

Douglas Farror, who spoke as he was rehabbing rental properties on Rosedale Avenue in Durham, is a case in point. "My background is not good," he says. "Felonies. Armed robbery. First-degree burglary." Farror served five and a half years. Surprisingly, his prison experience "wasn't awful," he says. While incarcerated, he went back to school and learned industrial maintenance and culinary skills. But once he was released, no one was willing to hire him—until he went to work for Builders of Hope.

Farror began with HopeWorks in April 2008 while living at the Raleigh Rescue Mission's shelter. He initially worked three to four days a week on framing before moving on to hanging cabinets, laying tile, painting, and trim work. In the beginning, each day presented him with the chance to acquire new skills and a sense of excitement over his steep learning curve. Now, he's more seasoned, and his satisfactions have mellowed and matured. "I have learned a whole lot here," he says brightly.

"I hold my head up high because of Builders of Hope"

Probably even more significant than the skill set Farror has acquired are the new relationships he has built, ones that have given him faith in humanity and instilled a newfound sense of self. "I hold my head up high because of Builders of Hope. I also want to mention Ben Britt and Chris Lewis, site supervisors. We bonded. Chris calls me all the time."

As a result of Farror's success in the work-mentor program, he was offered full-time employment upon graduation. Thanks to his steady paycheck, he's been able to move into his own apartment just three blocks from North Carolina Central University.

Ordinary things that most middle-class Americans take for granted are shining signals—and daily reminders—of just how far he has come. "I pay my bills and go buy groceries," he says with unmistakable pride. He is managing his money and has established a regular savings plan.

Michael White, 40, works alongside Douglas Farror restoring houses on Rosedale Avenue. Like Farror, White joined the BOH construction team through the HopeWorks program. He instantly found work he loves: demolition. He also discovered an appetite for doing what he calls "the hard work." "I like to go under houses and cut wires and take out what's there, whether it's scrap metal, scrap wire, or anything else."

Like Farror, White has seen his share of hard times. He did drugs for 20 years. He was out on the streets. He remembers the day when he got fed up with that life and decided to move in a new direction: August 31, 2007. Someone told him about the Durham Rescue Mission. "I was hungry and, at about 10:30 at night, I checked in." He was fed and assigned a bunk bed in the basement. After seven days there, during which time his system detoxed, he came to a realization. "I asked myself whether life was all about getting drunk and high. I made a decision to change my life."

Work-mentees at Barrington Village take a break from their deconstruction and demolition work.

He signed up for Encourager, a Christian program offered by the mission, one he now attends faithfully every week. At his very first meeting, he was asked by the group leader if he had been saved. "He told me about the Lord," White says. The leader invited him to join, a commitment that entailed six months of Bible study and work. After three weeks with Encourager, White was invited to move to the next level and enter the Victory Program, which, among other things, required him to quite literally clean up his act. For the first time in decades, he shaved and put on a coat and tie.

"I haven't been broke since"

Broke at the time, White remembers earning $20 for washing a woman's car. With that money, he bought a pack of cigarettes and realized that he was not even tempted to purchase drugs. "I haven't been broke since," he says. Today, White has both checking and savings accounts. He brandishes two uncashed checks, one for $300 and the second for $20. Maybe for the first time, life is good.

The road to a new life is rarely without frightening detours. Though he has never relapsed, White once experienced a crisis of temptation when he "wanted badly to get high." The desire was so strong that he had to get down on his knees and pray for 20 minutes to avoid doing something stupid. He thought of the people who had helped him whom he would disappoint if he fell off the drug-free wagon. Through summoning up the voices of his site supervisors and his aunts, as well as rallying the internal resources that were gaining strength inside him, he managed to come through the storm. "I woke up and felt better than I do today," he says.

White has managed to save up enough money to move into a Durham apartment of his own, with furniture supplied by the Durham Rescue Mission. He recently invited a number of co-workers over to show it off. "The first thing he did was take me to the cabinet in the kitchen and open the door," says BOH's Darryl Colwell, White's boss's boss. "It was full of groceries. He is so happy and proud to have a pantry stocked with food." Good things are now happening for White, all cascading from his resolve to get clean and sober, embrace faith, and commit to HopeWorks. Now that he has achieved his first few goals, he continues to set new ones. Next up: buying a used car. After that, he has set the longer-term goal of purchasing a house from Builders of Hope. To that end, he is working with a credit-counseling partner to establish a credit history. "He wants to qualify for a home in Durham," says Colwell. "I think he'll achieve it."

The Beginning: The First Partner

Uplifting stories like those of White, Farror, and Jones make it easy to understand how central the HopeWorks program is to the lives it touches and transforms, as well as to society at large. While the program's success now seems self-evident, getting it launched was far from easy.

When Nancy Welsh started the work-mentor program, her first objective was to find viable mentees. To that end, she decided to seek out a like-minded agency that could be a solid partner. The Raleigh Rescue Mission, which enjoys a sterling reputation in the Triangle, came to mind.

Lynn Daniell, the mission's executive director, vividly recalls his first encounter with Welsh back in 2007. She had cold-called him to request a meeting. He was expecting a housing authority employee or a church person and was startled when an attractive, energetic woman appeared at his office. She opened the meeting, he recalls, by complimenting his program: "'I have so much respect for the Raleigh Rescue Mission.'" She then went on to share her plans for developing an affordable housing community comprised of recycled homes: "'Part of my goal is to find an agency with men who are in rehab and give them the opportunity to help someone else. Is this something you might be interested in?'" Daniell thought of a number of men at his mission who in better times had worked as carpenters, electricians, and painters and who needed to get their lives back on track. Many had basic construction skills. Some had "the gift." Why not put them to work?

In his many years at the mission, he had seen a lot of high-minded ideas, most of which never came to fruition. But Welsh gave him confidence. "With Nancy, I could tell from the start this was something different." He singles out one factor: her faith. "This was not all about Nancy, but about doing what God had called her to do." Tapping into his experience with start-up programs, Daniell signed on to help. "I have always been able to take a vision and make it happen," he says.

Growing Pains

When construction began on Builders of Hope's flagship community, the Raleigh Rescue Mission provided trainees who were willing to work. Welsh expected everyone in the field to be as excited with the new helpers as she and Lynn Daniell were. Straightaway, however, she encountered "pushback," as site supervisors proved reluctant to take on the trainees, viewing them as obstacles to progress.

Not long after Lew Schulman starting work for BOH in March 2008 as its chief financial officer (he subsequently assumed the role of president), he intervened. "The first thing I did was made sure that the construction manager and site supervisor understood that this was going to happen whether they wanted it to or not," he says. In fact, Welsh credits Schulman with evolving HopeWorks into what she calls "a functional, dynamic, integral component" of the construction process. "Lew was instrumental in making this happen."

A volunteer works with mentees from the Raleigh Rescue Mission.

Part of Schulman's effectiveness was his understanding of the source of reluctance on the part of construction crew members. "In the for-profit world, it's hard to persuade subcontractors to take on work-mentees," he says. "When you have already costed-out a project and have gotten it as a result of the bid you made, you're not interested in slowing the process by taking time out to train someone." The challenge was in demonstrating to the construction crew that Builders of Hope's paradigm was entirely different.

"A different flow and attitude on the construction site"

Ironically, though BOH employees were not bound under those traditional for-profit financial constraints, they brought with them a "get-'er-done" mentality that had to undergo a shift in order to embrace the work-mentor program. A big part of the educational process was impressing upon the construction crew that taking time out to train others wasn't an interruption of their job but rather *part* of the job. They had to wrap their arms around Builders of Hope's holistic approach. Yes, it was about saving buildings, but it was also about rebuilding lives. "We have a different flow and attitude on the construction site than the normal high-energy homebuilder," observes Alex Henzel.

Henzel came to work for Builders of Hope in August 2009 and was soon tasked with the mission of professionalizing the HopeWorks program. He set about developing and refining the program into a prototype that could be used at all of BOH's increasingly scattered work sites and replicated across the country. An engineer by training, Henzel drew on his background to inject uniformity and consistency into the format and to structure the program. He laid out on paper precisely what was to be expected of mentees and the consequences of straying from those guidelines. The concepts have been incorporated into a kind of handbook that is referenced by mentors and mentees whenever the need arises.

One of the first major changes was to extend the program term. Starting with its new class of mentees in January 2010, the work-mentor program doubled in length, from three to six months. BOH principals realized a half-year period was needed for the program to be truly transformational. "It takes three months just to get to know the individual and build loyalty," says Darryl Colwell.

Identifying the Right People

While program structure serves to keep everyone on course, probably the single most significant factor for achieving success is identifying the right people—both candidates who are ready to commit to growth and change and patient, caring employees who are prepared to teach, nurture, and bring them along. To that end, the organization goes to lengths to select individuals who are cut out to serve as mentors. During the recent downturn, Builders of Hope has had its pick of employees. "When we put out our ads for site supervisors, we got guys who were making $150,000 a year supervising construction sites applying," says Henzel. "We didn't hire them because the minute the economy picks up, they'll be gone." Instead, the organization set its sights on finding "special people"—those genuinely committed to the mission, who would therefore be likely to stay with Builders of Hope for the long haul.

Once the right people are in place, the next step is fostering strong one-on-one relationships between workers in training and the site supervisors or assistant site supervisors who serve as mentors. "We know from experience that our mentees need lots of attention, positive feedback, and tender loving care," says Colwell. To maximize the time and attention paid to each one, the organization whenever possible assigns no more than three mentees to each mentor; two are even better. Experience has taught the organization that if too many mentees are taken on, they can get lost in the crowd, compromising program effectiveness.

Working with Existing Programs

All HopeWorks trainees come through one of several programs provided by partnering organizations. Builders of Hope partners with departments of corrections, homeless shelters, rescue missions, and other entities that are engaged in job- and life-skills training programs for those with barriers to employment. "We like to dovetail off of existing programs," says Lew Schulman. "That way, we can focus on what we do best." What Builders of Hope uniquely brings to the table is its work program. While some provide complementary and necessary skills, "the work component is invariably missing" from other social reentry programs.

The Raleigh Rescue Mission, for example, offers a yearlong program that focuses on getting participants healthy physically and mentally while endowing them with a variety of real-world skills that will enable them to integrate into mainstream society. "We teach responsibility and life skills," says Lynn Daniell, "in preparation for moving them into what Builders of Hope does."

Work-Mentor Candidates: "An infinite waiting list"

Because work-training programs for ex-offenders and others with barriers to employment are few and far between, candidates work hard to get into the program and to stay once they are in. "We have an infinite waiting list," says Lew Schulman. "There are always people waiting—more than we could possibly hire," Alex Henzel concurs. About the only "negative" to his job as manager of social programs "is that once people learn about HopeWorks, everyone wants to get on board. You hate to turn people away, but you have to."

The requirements for HopeWorks work-mentor candidates are more stringent for some partnering entities than others, but all organizations supplying BOH with program trainees retain some presence in their candidates' lives after placement. That—along with in-house requirements and such "wraparound services" as meals, housing, drug treatment, and life skills classes—provide some measure of assurance that the candidates will be successful.

The bar set by the North Carolina Department of Corrections (DOC) in Charlotte, for example, is one of the highest among the organizations with which BOH works. "We asked them to bring in a pool of candidates for the five work-mentor positions we had to fill," says Colwell. DOC narrowed its list of qualified applicants to 15 names, then winnowed it down to 10 strong prospects, from which BOH selected five. Just to make it to the point of being interviewed, the candidates had to clear many hurdles. "They have to be free of drugs for a number of months, which is determined by rigorous drug testing," Colwell says. "My understanding is that the DOC has a one-strike rule. Anyone who strays can go back to jail because these folks are on probation." What's more, DOC's baseline educational requirement is that all candidates must complete their GED certificate before entering the program.

From 10 such carefully screened candidates, how was the Builders of Hope team able to pick the winners? "What we're listening for—and what we want to hear—is that they truly have an interest in this industry," says Colwell. Not surprisingly, candidates with construction experience get a leg up.

In addition to those who have a desire to work in construction, BOH tries to pick people it believes will succeed, Henzel says. "We don't want to waste our resources on someone who's in it for what they'll get for the moment."

Interviewers set the tone for future success by demonstrating sensitivity and making a point not to ask questions about the candidates' past transgressions. "No questions are asked about incarceration or anything that might potentially embarrass them," says Schulman. "We want to put our candidates at ease." The same courtesies apply once the mentees come onto the job.

"The sparkle in their eyes"

The combination of the reconfigured program, with its stringent requirements and rigorous benchmarks, and the candidates' own commitment and enthusiasm has led Colwell to predict great things from the newest class of work-mentees. Early indicators certainly point that way. So far in Charlotte, the DOC trainees and all workers have proven exceptionally reliable. "I don't know if we've had one call in sick yet after four months on the job," says

Colwell. "They all arrive on time at 8 A.M. They're excited each day they come in. You can see the sparkle in their eyes. They're hard, hard workers. The success rate is going to be huge."

While some of the nonprofit's other partners aren't quite as strict as the Department of Corrections—for example, the rescue missions in Raleigh and Durham don't require a GED certificate prior to placement—all offer structured programs, including drug, alcohol, and financial counseling, from which the participants benefit. "We have many different partners," says Colwell. "They all fill needs in the communities in many different ways."

Orientation: "If they're not giving 100 percent, they're gone"

On their first day on the job, all work-mentees are given an orientation to the Builders of Hope world. The mentor sits down with the new hire or group of hires and lays out the basic ground rules and expectations for success at Builders of Hope.

Call it a "tough love" approach, but it works. "If we lay out our expectations very clearly from day one," says Lew Schulman, "there is very little correction that we have to make. What we want to impress upon them from the beginning is that we're not a lunch stop. If they're not giving 100 percent, they're gone."

Following are some of the rules that the mentees are presented at their orientation session.

1. Work hours are 8:00 A.M. to 4:30 P.M. Monday through Friday. (Occasionally, the schedule is adjusted based on transit-line schedules.)

2. Show up for work on time. Pay will be docked and a fine will be levied for an unexcused late arrival.

3. Work hard during work hours but relax during the two 15-minute breaks (in the morning and afternoon) and at the half-hour lunch break.

4. If for any reason you can't make it to work, notify your site supervisor immediately.

These dilapidated rental units on State Street in Raleigh, North Carolina, were eyesores.

They bred drug activity, prostitution, and violence and were easy targets for graffiti and guns.

Photos by Jessie Gladin-Kramer
Captions by Anne-Marie Vanaman

People found it hard to take pride in the places they called home.

State Street was the place your mother warned you never to go—unless you lived there.

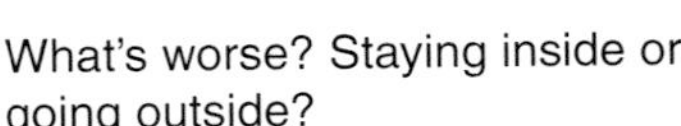

What's worse? Staying inside or going outside?

Americans spend 90 percent of their time indoors and are exposed to air pollutants and common allergens such as mold. Much “affordable” housing has multiple health and safety issues that directly affect residents.

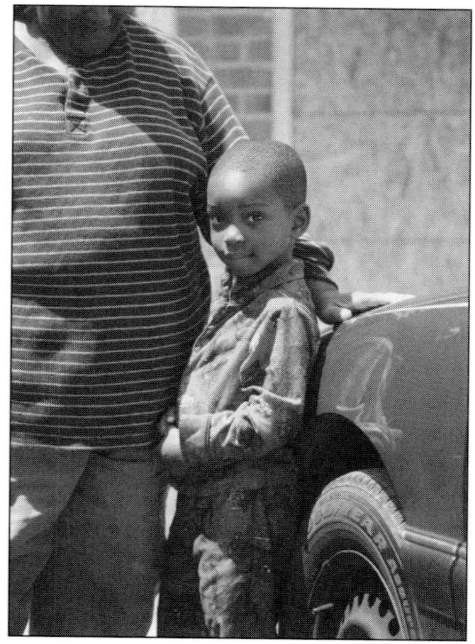

Young children are especially vulnerable to indoor-air illnesses such as asthma. In fact, approximately 40 percent of diagnosed asthma in children is believed to be caused by indoor air pollution.

Living in neighborhoods prone to crime and isolated from strong social networks contributes to psychological distress that can manifest itself as anxiety, depression, or aggression. This resident talked about her community's problems as she walked down State Street.

In spite of overwhelming obstacles in their surroundings, many residents made their apartments as cozy as possible.

In the summer of 2010, Builders of Hope acquired the State Street Villas. The transformation began with a hammer.

Who didn't like to knock over building blocks as a child? A volunteer group begins interior deconstruction on the apartments.

It typically takes Builders of Hope 90 days to rehabilitate and green a home.

Approximately 65 percent of the existing structure is reused, resulting in lower construction costs and saving tons of debris from landfills.

Like many cities, Raleigh experienced pockets of revitalization. However, developers demolished many structures like the State Street apartments and replaced them with housing too expensive for the original residents, thereby displacing them from their communities permanently.

Builders of Hope commits to offering housing to the community's original residents first. No one is displaced.

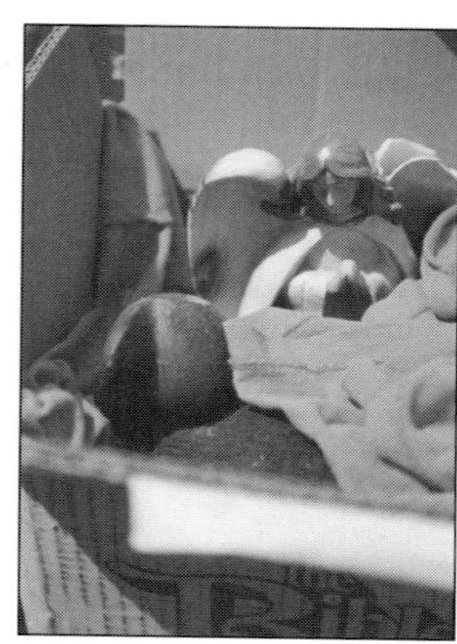

An angel's temporary home

When drywall is removed, little or no insulation may be found, as is not uncommon in "affordable housing."

Housing with no moisture barriers and poor insulation can lead to chronic dampness and mold.

Here, the subfloor was so damp that weeds could be seen growing inside.

Broken appliances, high energy bills, bug infestations, mold, and poor insulation were typical problems on State Street. Here, insects have taken over a kitchen sink.

Left behind: in spite of substandard conditions and a dangerous neighborhood, lives were lived and children were loved dearly.

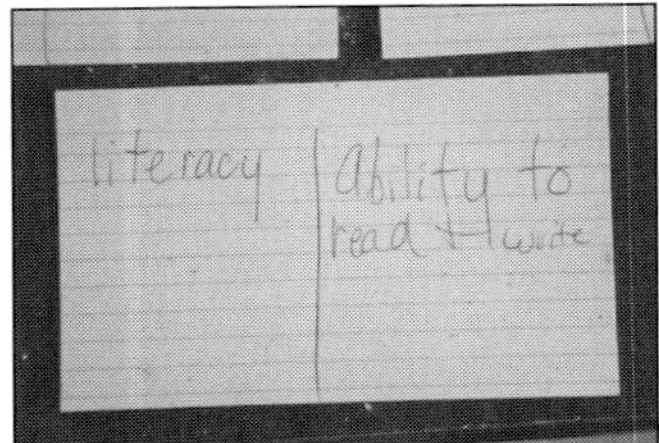

A child's vocabulary homework saved from the rubble

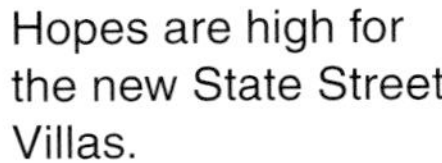

Hopes are high for the new State Street Villas.

Living space is already brighter and cleaner. This resident is thrilled with her new wall-mounted, energy-efficient air conditioner, a standard feature in the State Street Villas.

A relocated tenant peers into his new, clean, energy-efficient stove and admires the bamboo flooring and wood cabinets. No particle board here.

Here, residents are getting familiar with higher standards—Builders of Hope standards. Among those standards are sustainably grown wood and tile flooring, Craftsman styling, low-VOC paint, and high-efficiency heating and cooling.

Before

Already, the change is significant.

Like an old home, a community can have good bones. Builders of Hope realizes a community's single greatest resource is its people.

Through the HopeWorks mentor program, individuals with barriers to employment, such as those recovering from addiction, are given a second chance.

Doug Farror stepped up to the HopeWorks challenge and transformed his life. After graduating from the six-month program, he was hired by the Builders of Hope construction team in Raleigh, North Carolina. He has an easy commute. He became one of the first tenants in the State Street Villas—which he helped build.

Doug Farror and David Welsh, vice president of property management for Builders of Hope, discuss the positive change the community is already experiencing.

Two participants in the HopeWorks mentor program take a break to survey their work.

Rebuilt with sustainability in mind, the State Street Villas meet LEED Gold criteria and guarantee affordable energy bills. Tenants pay below-market rates, so they have more money left over at the end of the month for other necessities, such as food and health care.

Affordable homes that don't look, or live, like affordable housing

Home is more than shelter. It is a haven for family and dreams.

The last nail has been hammered, the shovels put away.

For Doug, a home and a new chance at life. For Raleigh, a more vibrant community.

Rebuilding Homes.
Revitalizing Communities.
Transforming Lives.

5. Every morning, meet with your mentor to review the day's expectations and discuss the previous day's progress.
6. Appropriate appearance is required. ("No identifying colors or clothing with profanity or any inflammatory sayings will be tolerated," the handbook states.)
7. Every Friday, participate in a weekly evaluation.
8. Causes for immediate termination are theft, carrying a weapon, engaging in an altercation with anyone at the job site, and failure to adhere to the alcohol and drug policy. (Random drug tests are performed at least twice during the six-month term.)

Weekly Evaluation: "A sharing feedback session"

Every Friday, generally in the morning, each mentee meets with his mentor in the construction office or at some other quiet place away from the hubbub for what Colwell calls "a sharing feedback session." These face-to-face sit-down meetings can last anywhere from 15 minutes to an hour, depending on the agenda. Instead of dreading this time, most mentees look forward to their weekly sessions, Colwell has observed. The structured blocks of time put the complete focus on mentees, who crave feedback, constructive criticism, and recognition for jobs well done. "Growing up, most of these individuals never had much positive reinforcement," he says. "They want to know how they did, good or bad—what they need to work on and what they did right."

Each mentor acts as a kind of coach who encourages and cheers on his charges not only in honing their work skills ("always measure twice before you cut") but in developing such basic workplace competencies as appropriate communications and problem-solving skills. How, for instance, can a mentee learn to respectfully disagree with a fellow employee or even his superior? The feedback sessions might include prompting from the mentor on specific language the mentees could use in such situations to state their position, and how to back down respectfully if they're overruled. Teamwork, respect for authority, and conflict resolution are key areas covered. While construction training gives participants the skills and experience to qualify for real-world jobs, their life-skills work gives them the capacity to maintain their positions.

Such sessions helped Douglas Farror learn the importance of being considerate and appreciative of coworkers. "I've learned to be respectful of others. I've learned to be on time. I've learned discipline." After every weekly session, the mentors write up reports, which are placed in the mentees' permanent files. But Colwell stresses that it is the interaction, not the written reports, that counts most.

The Work They Do

Once the parameters of the job have been defined and the ground rules established, what sorts of tasks do the mentees actually perform? They start out with the basics—that is, the time-consuming daily tasks involved with keeping the work site safe, clean, and ready for business. Every morning, the mentees are involved in setup. They unlock doors and open windows. They open containers and bring out tools. Workers sweep floors, porches, and driveways and remove debris. The procedure is repeated in reverse at the end of each day. They put away tools, set aside recyclable material for future use, toss nonrecyclable debris into dumpsters, and secure doors and windows for the night.

From the get-go, mentees start performing what Lew Schulman calls "meaningful work," acquiring skill sets that will be valuable in the future. The skills are introduced gradually, so site supervisors have time to teach the work-safety protocols involved with each task, especially regarding the use of power tools. Until the mentees earn their stripes, he says, they are not assigned "aesthetically obvious" jobs such as trim work and painting.

Because the houses donated to Builders of Hope must be retrofitted with wiring, plumbing, and insulation, the first order of business when a "new" house arrives on-site is deconstruction. To that end, the first real "construction" job most mentees are assigned is demolition work. After the gutting is complete, their initiation into reconstruction begins with basic framing. Mentees start by assisting with such jobs as framing out windows and doors. After assisting for a period of time—on average, three months—they start to perform such work on their own. Likewise, they are gradually introduced to the use of power tools and are given what Colwell calls such "basic fine-tuning" tasks as replacing screw plates in doors and installing doorknobs and light-plate switches. Other common jobs at this stage include applying silicon caulking to seal air leaks in cracks and crevices and building temporary handrails on the porches and temporary stairs to the houses. During the course of the six-month training, they participate in virtually every aspect of deconstruction and reconstruction of rescued homes, so they come out with thorough knowledge of the complete building assembly process.

In addition to construction, the mentees are heavily engaged in landscaping work. They lay sod and plant shrubs and trees. (Each Builders of Hope home is blessed with one flowering tree and one hardwood tree.) They work on contouring yards and preparing drainage plateaus to direct rainwater away from the houses.

Workers' Progress

As the program hums along, it becomes obvious which workers will progress quickly and which ones will need more time. Members of the management team at Builders of Hope recognize that not all mentees are created equal. Some acquire skills more rapidly than others. Some will need two months to master a skill that others pick up in two weeks. Mentees are never terminated for being slow, says Lew Schulman. "The goal is not to measure them

Kennie Bynum, one of Builders of Hope's first work-mentees, is now a full-time employee. (Photo by Jennifer Kromhout)

based on aptitude, but on effort." What matters most to managers is that everyone is moving forward and making progress.

During the course of the program, certain aptitudes and interests emerge among the mentees. Kennie Bynum, a former work-mentee who was once homeless and struggled with drug and alcohol addiction, developed a strong interest in laying tile. In fact, he learned to lay tile with such proficiency—and loved it so much—that when he graduated from the work-mentor program, he was hired full time as a "tile guy." In the world of Builders of Hope, Kennie Bynum is a superstar.

Treating Mentees As "Regular Employees"

A large factor in the success of the program is introducing mentees to the realities of the world of work. To that end, Builders of Hope has created a learning environment that provides teachable moments at every turn, along with real-world rewards for playing by the rules.

Mentees are treated as "regular employees," says Henzel, and are encouraged to dress professionally and behave appropriately in the field. "If you look the part and act the part," he counsels, "it's a whole lot easier to get people to believe you." It is also easier for mentees to believe in themselves. Mentees are paid real wages, starting at $8 per hour, with the opportunity for merit raises. "If they work hard, we may increase them to $10 an hour," he says. "It shows the other participants that if they hustle, they, too, can get rewarded." Mentees are also given paid sick days, paid holidays, and time off for doctors' visits and meetings with parole officers.

Despite the care with which the program was crafted, it is not always smooth sailing for mentees or staff. "These guys require more than the average guy," says Henzel. "They're going to make mistakes. They have social problems, interaction problems. They may not know how to react after being incarcerated so many years, or how to talk to the supervisor."

Another challenge that BOH staffers have encountered with mentees is difficulty submitting to authority. On occasion, mentees have been known to step over the line and try winging a job to prove to their supervisors that they can do it on their own. "We'll take him aside and say, 'You're not in charge here. We tell you how to do this. Chill out and be the student here,'" Henzel says. "From the employer/mentor side, you have to think of these missteps as part of the growth process. These people are growing, and with that growth comes mistakes." Whatever the reasons for the transgressions, mentees need a clear line across which they dare not step.

In his previous work as a general contractor, Chris Lewis primarily built custom homes. In the for-profit world, if a subcontract employee messes up—say, by cutting a two-by-four short—he has to cover the replacement cost, Lewis says. At Builders of Hope, where Lewis works as a construction site supervisor, it simply slows the pace of progress when something similar happens. The trainee is never charged for the material. "What matters is teaching them how to do it right," he says. In the field, Lewis supervises Michael White and Doug Farror, whom he calls "good workers." He has taken pride in watching both men develop, become more responsible, and find "a purpose to what they do."

Though the program has proven largely successful, Builders of Hope on occasion has had to dismiss mentees for theft or drug use. And it has also encountered a few slackers who wanted to coast through without expending much effort. For his part, though, Henzel says he sleeps well at night for helping provide an opportunity. "If they don't follow through, at least you know you gave them a chance."

Impacting Fellow BOH Employees, Volunteers, and the Community

The HopeWorks program powerfully impacts everyone it touches, Builders of Hope's own employees included. "There's a personal satisfaction you get from helping so many people," says Chris Lewis, who has worked for the nonprofit since October 2008. Though Lewis's previous work was far more lucrative, his present position offers a different kind of reward. "To see the first-time homeowner come in and be blown away means so much. And nothing compares to watching mentees develop and become more responsible. It's not only good for the environment, it's good for the guys who work here, giving them jobs down the road."

Alex Henzel uses stronger language to describe the contrast between his former life in the for-profit world as a senior project manager at a manufacturing company and his work overseeing the work-mentor and youth-build programs. "I came out of an intensively stressful career. Of course, I was paid extremely well, but there's a penalty you pay for that salary: the stress, the backstabbing, the nastiness." Henzel characterizes the atmosphere at Builders of Hope as peaceful, one in which employees work together toward common goals. In his previous life, "everyone was out for themselves," he says. "Here, no one is out for themselves. They're out to make things happen."

This "we're all in it together" attitude affects not only those out in the field working alongside mentees but also white-collar workers in the home office, including those who sell houses, raise funds, and provide legal and administrative services. Nancy Welsh understands that while Builders of Hope salaries will never make her employees rich, the work itself is endowed with meaning, as well as the chance to blaze a trail and the opportunity to contribute to something larger than themselves. "It's not just the ex-offenders and work-mentors who are impacted. All of us are changed by what we do at Builders of Hope," she says. Welsh still pinches herself when she hears testimonials from employees about how their lives have been positively impacted by their work. A case in point is the following e-mail—written by the organization's director of sales—which recently landed in the CEO's inbox.

> Nancy—
>
> I just got out of my presentation and had to drop you an e-mail. I just wanted to let you know what an absolute honor it is helping you fulfill your vision through Builders of Hope. My eyes are tearing as I reflect on what a humbling and enlightening experience tonight was.

> I gave a presentation to members of MCE [Middle Class Express] for their motivational meeting. Afterwards, I had woman after woman come up to me to share a piece of her life journey and struggle. So many said they believed BOH was a gift sent from God. I met Tiwana, whose 15-year-old daughter was recently sexually assaulted and [is] now pregnant, and a 56-year-old whose grandson is chronically ill from the mold he inhaled as an infant in their overpriced rental.
>
> It is easy to get caught up in the daily business of closings, real-estate agents, and financial transactions. I am so grateful to have had the chance to reconnect tonight. I met so many beautiful people, and I will do everything I can to help them through BOH and our partnerships. And I just want to let you know how grateful I am for you and this opportunity, if I don't tell you enough.
>
> Lindsay [Lindsay L. Locke, director of sales, Builders of Hope]

"Everything that you've been through, don't keep it as a chip on your shoulder; keep it as a feather in your cap."

—Nancy Welsh's counsel to work-mentees

The Power of Giving Back

An important ingredient in the formula undergirding the success of the HopeWorks program is its call for mentees to step up to the plate to give back. "Giving of themselves to make a difference for others," says Welsh, "is an integral part of their transformation." This simple step enables mentees to grow beyond the state of victimhood into full human beings who give as well as receive—who by reaching out to feel others' pain find their own diminished.

Mentees are encouraged to form bonds and share stories and cautionary wisdom with at-risk youth and others. Welsh counsels them to tap past torments as a source of strength. "Everything that you've been through, don't keep it as a chip on your shoulder; keep it as a feather in your cap," she will say. "Having been through the wringer gives you the privilege to speak to these kids on a level that I don't have, because I haven't been there." Once mentees open up, they commonly make comments like, "You don't want to go to jail, where I was." Another expectation is that once mentees make it through the program, they'll become mentors themselves. Who could be better? "They can share their experience," says Henzel. "They can say, 'You want to have what I have? You *can* make it. You *will* make it.'"

Builders of Hope managers understand the healing power that sharing their stories holds for mentees. To that end, they promote mentee interaction with members of the news media, funders, volunteers, homebuyers, and curious neighbors and onlookers who come out to learn more about the miracles spun by the organization. Not only does this testimony help mentees, it in turn serves to give back to the organization by spreading the word.

Building the At-Risk Youth Program

Matching adult mentees with troubled youth has proven to be an effective piece of Builders of Hope's At-Risk Youth program. Now that the adult program is up and running so smoothly, managers are training their focus on bringing the youth program up to speed as well. In the past, the program has produced mixed results. Welsh points with pride to a few memorable moments, such as when a group of female youth-mentees worked hard and proved to be "better than the guys." But on another occasion, Builders of Hope took on too many youth-mentees while lacking an adequate number of adults to serve them. "We ended up being babysitters," admits Henzel.

In Charlotte, BOH principals see a new chapter ahead for the At-Risk Youth program. Henzel has developed a partnership with an area high school that focuses on at-risk youth, including those from troubled homes and those facing mental challenges. The new approach? Builders of Hope made a strategic decision to keep the numbers low for maximum impact. It starts with a more manageable-sized group of youth-mentees and requires the school to provide on-site chaperons to supervise and direct the students. Now that the program has been up and running for six months, Henzel is happy to report that it is proving successful and fostering real change in the children. BOH staffers are excited to see how it turns out because "no one has ever given these kids real work," Henzel says.

One Student's Turnaround

Alex Henzel treasures turnaround stories. One of his favorites involves a 17-year-old student named Gerard who made enormous strides in the At-Risk Youth program. During the boy's graduation ceremony, which was held at the Rowan Apartments in Charlotte, Henzel was conversing with the head of the school system's Occupational Community Service program when Gerard approached them. "'Mr. Alex,'" Henzel remembers him saying, "'so sorry to bother you. I just wanted to talk to you. I'll catch you later on.'" The OCS director—who was seeing the BOH program for the first time—did a double take. She told Henzel, "I don't believe what I just heard. That boy is *the most problematic child* in the school system. How did he become so polite?" Henzel explained to her how the program worked and how the mentees learned many skills, including respect.

He references Gerard's polite interjection as an "aha" moment for the OCS director, who in a heartbeat—in Malcolm Gladwell's proverbial "blink"—bought into the Builders of Hope program.

The Magic of the HopeWorks Program

The simple words *real work* are the key to the success—the magic, if you will—of HopeWorks. The Builders of Hope program—maybe for the first time—has given members of challenged populations the opportunity to find real work for themselves, work in which they can develop their character, personal discipline, viable marketplace skills, and a place for themselves in society and the world.

"This program has grown to something more than I could have ever imagined," says Alex Henzel. "We are literally watching change in front of our eyes." Often when work-mentees come through the door for their interviews or the first day on the job,

Hard work pays off. Mentees celebrate on graduation day.

they lack self-esteem, he observes. If they have worked, they have probably held down only "crummy, horrible jobs." A case in point is an older trainee who had never done anything more meaningful than scrubbing toilets and washing pots. "When he came for the interview, his head was down, submissive. It was, 'Yes, sir. No, sir.'" Now that the trainee has successfully completed the HopeWorks work-mentor program with Builders of Hope, Henzel has seen a complete transformation. The same man now walks around with "a bit of a swagger" because he has learned a strong new set of skills, is making a contribution, and is treated respectfully in his community. Perhaps as important as anything else, he has embraced an attitude of gratitude for the new lease on life that he has been given and that he has accepted so well.

Builders of Hope employees and volunteers are constantly inspired when they witness such remarkable transformations and see lives, including their own, touched and changed. Henzel puts it best: "How can you not have fun doing this work and changing people's lives?"

CHAPTER 5

THE PARTNERSHIP PRINCIPLE

Partnership stands at the center of every successful solutions-based social entrepreneurial effort, and few organizations demonstrate its primacy and effectiveness better than Builders of Hope. Identifying "the win" for its partners is a core principle that guides and informs the organization; it's a concept that has paved the way for its explosive growth. This examination of an array of Builders of Hope's partners and stakeholders—from house donors to educational institutions to government entities—brings the nonprofit to life and offers insight into the nuts and bolts of the organization.

Partnerships: Win-Win Solutions

Builders of Hope CEO Nancy Welsh takes to partnership like a duck to water, and her example sets the bar to which her employees aspire. "The strength of our company—or any company—can be measured by the strength of its partnerships," she says.

So what exactly is a healthy partnership? Welsh answers without hesitation: "It is a relationship in which each party is able to contribute significantly with something they have expertise in, without impeding upon the expertise of another. It's playing on your strengths and using your strengths to enhance the greater good."

When building her organization, Welsh drew on the wisdom and knowledge base of many others. "Many hands make light work," she says. Her first Builders of Hope partnership was with John Jenkins, a builder who taught her the basic art, craft, and business of construction and rehab and was the organization's first employee. Many other partnerships with individuals and organizations followed. Establishing and tapping into partnerships remain fundamental to understanding the fast-growing organization. "Partners are like pieces of the puzzle when you're creating a masterwork," Welsh says. "Without all those pieces, you end up with holes."

"The urge to form partnerships, to link up in collaborative arrangements, is perhaps the oldest, strongest, and most fundamental force in nature. There are no solitary, free-living creatures: every form of life is dependent on other forms."

—Lewis Thomas

Instead of "re-creating the wheel" when she started HopeWorks, the organization's work-mentor program, Welsh looked toward a program already in place at the Raleigh Rescue Mission. (It helped that she was already a trusted member of the RRM family, sitting on its board of directors.) Rather than copying or competing with the existing program, Welsh opted to partner with RRM by inviting its trainees to join forces with Builders of Hope. "It's a matter of finding partners who do what they do and do it really well, which increases the strength of the core."

Watching Nancy Welsh in action shows how "the partnership principle" translates into real life. In almost every arena into which she steps, she scans the landscape looking for synergies, partnership opportunities that could benefit her organization as well as the other party. Many of those meetings and opportunities she creates herself.

For example, when the nonprofit was getting off the ground back in 2006, Welsh set up a meeting with the Raleigh division manager of General Shale Brick, Alex Allen, to describe the Builders of Hope model. Purpose of the visit: to invite his company's participation. Coming from the world of business, Welsh guessed (correctly) that General Shale Brick might have excess inventory—cosmetically questionable but structurally sound bricks—that could be put to good use as foundational pieces where such aesthetics as "perfection" and "consistency" were not of paramount importance.

While the company can sometimes sell its brick seconds, it is forced in many cases to crush them for use in landscaping or to send them directly to the landfill. Welsh came up with a win-win solution for General Shale Brick and Builders of Hope. The company could play an important role in making a difference in the world while putting its imperfect product to good use, gaining tax advantages, and generating goodwill. General Shale Brick agreed to donate brick seconds to Builders of Hope for a prototype home in its debut community, Barrington Village.

"When you see brick, you think quality."

—Nancy Welsh

"Right from the start, I wanted to use brick on our Builders of Hope houses," says Welsh, "but this high-quality product was out of our low-budget price range. Brick embodies the solidity and permanence that I want our communities to represent. When you see brick, you think quality." Her vision for the community included the liberal and visible use of brick on the foundations and at the bases of the substantial columns on the front porches. These solid columns compare favorably visually and structurally to the spindly two-by-four rails that are standard in many other affordable housing projects. What's more, brick-based columns encourage the porch-based community life that the organization actively promotes.

Not only did Welsh home in on a specific material that could make a difference in the look and feel of Builders of Hope's first community, she deliberated long and hard over the scope of her "ask" to her potential donor and was careful not to "over-ask." In that introductory meeting with Alex Allen, she did not request brick for entire houses but rather invited the company to donate material for these critical components of each home.

After work was completed on the first batch of houses, Alex Allen came out to the Barrington construction site at Welsh's invitation. He liked what he saw and agreed to donate brick for the entire 24-home community. "He said, 'Okay. Pick your colors.'" Welsh remembers the company's donation as a milestone in upgrading the "construction values" for the community, as well as an auspicious omen of the many successful partnerships in the offing. "It was awesome," she recalls.

Gifts in Kind

Aware of the sheer quantity of usable—and often new—inventory that is sent to the landfill, Builders of Hope associates vowed to tap this resource to outfit homes. One of the first programs the organization signed up for was Gifts In Kind International, a dispenser of surplus goods to nonprofits. The way it works is this: the recipient organization accepts whatever is donated. "When you accept a donation, they won't tell you much about what you'll get or how you're going to get it," Welsh explains.

One of Builders of Hope's first and most memorable gifts was $400,000 worth of lighting, at a cost of $500 for shipping. The bonanza turned out to be predominantly *commercial* fixtures. Welsh and her staff realized they had a valuable resource, but how to use it? The organization had no need for commercial lighting for its houses, so Welsh did some creative thinking. Aware of a nearby church building under construction, she asked around and found out that funding had dried up and the project was in need of the lighting. She realized the church had excess capacity in its warehouse. Welsh proposed a swap. In exchange for donating the lighting fixtures, Builders of Hope could use the warehouse to store its growing inventory. It was a win-win situation and represented the ultimate partnership: two entities helping each other, both saving money.

Since that auspicious beginning, the organization has continued to develop key partnerships that effectively trim the bottom line. Businesses routinely donate new and discontinued merchandise to the nonprofit in exchange for tax deductions. Raleigh's Home Depot megastore donates "open-container stuff"—unsold inventory in pristine condition—along with other items. Off the top of her head, Welsh ticks off a list of items now in BOH storage that were donated through Home Depot's Framing Hope program: seven toilets, 100 doorbells, and a stack of shiny brass house numbers. She can't keep track of it all.

The Common Ground Green Building Center in Durham chips in whenever it can. Though its price points are often higher than the nonprofit can afford, the group occasionally offers up deals to Builders of Hope when it gets overstocks of paint. "We keep them top of mind," says co-owner Paul Toma. "Recently, we had an opportunity where a distributor was trying to get rid of paint stock. We turned around and called Builders of Hope and asked if they'd be interested. I do whatever I can to help them out."

Builders of Hope's latest corporate partnership is with Lowe's Home Improvement stores. Already, Lowe's Charitable and Educational Foundation has made a substantial grant to BOH, and the nonprofit is currently in discussions to expand the partnership.

A Multitude of Partners

General Shale Brick is but one of a multitude of partners Builders of Hope has teamed up with in its short life. These partnerships encompass a full spectrum of players: from its clients (the homebuyers and renters) to its employees (most of whom gravitate toward the organization for its mission-based work); from its financial partners (such as banks and lenders) to housing and credit-counseling agencies (whose employees identify and counsel potential homebuyers and renters about qualifying for affordable housing programs). Builders of Hope's partnership tentacles reach toward its institutional partners—colleges and universities with which it works on experiments in green living, solar power innovation, and rehab. (Two of BOH's most notable partners are the North Carolina Solar Center and Advanced Energy.) The spectrum includes governmental partners at the local, state, and federal levels—which are critical in identifying the needs and resources of an area—as well as volunteers, schools, day cares, community centers, and religious communities.

A former women's crew coach at Duke University, Emily Egge came to work for Builders of Hope in 2008, writing grants and helping establish the organization's first development department. Egge speaks to the profound impact that Welsh's partnership orientation has had on her approach to her own work. "I have come to realize that every facet of our lives is connected through people, through interactions, through geography," Egge says. "Working for Builders of Hope has made me look for connections in a different way—for the less obvious."

Among the "less obvious" partnerships are ones Egge has helped create with Raleigh-area educational institutions such as the University of North Carolina at Chapel Hill, North Carolina State University, Duke University, St. Augustine's College, and others. For instance, Egge has helped coordinate with graduate schools the use of BOH programs and projects as "case studies." In effect, the effort has engaged enterprising grad students as pro bono consultants to study BOH projects and make outside-the-box recommendations. One such program set up with UNC–Chapel Hill grad students analyzed the HopeWorks work-mentor program. Area colleges and universities also consistently contribute interns to the BOH offices.

> *"Mirror your partner's dreams;
> the relationship will grow."*
>
> **—Unknown**

A Win for Both Parties: The Ticket to Partnership

One reason partnerships work so well for Builders of Hope is that the organization's employees strive to protect the interests of its partners. Welsh works to understand what will motivate her partners before she comes to the table. "I don't walk into a meeting without knowing what the win is for the other person, and how I can get them to where they're going. I need to know what they're looking for." Through her many business dealings, Welsh has observed that people often tell what they want, but it's really not what they want at all. "Not everyone is solution-driven," she says. "Part of finding out what they want is figuring out what they need."

For instance, if an entity seeks to donate a number of properties to Builders of Hope, the first job for the organization is to determine the motivation of its prospective partner. What problem is the donation solving for this group? Is this company carrying notes? Is it having trouble selling the properties? "Once you figure out the motivation," says Welsh, "you can get creative in helping to solve problems and find solutions."

> *"Not everyone is solution-driven. Part of finding out
> what they want is figuring out what they need."*
>
> **—Nancy Welsh**

Sometimes, in the interest of serving their partners, Builders of Hope principals give *more* than was initially agreed upon. This approach surprises—even stuns—many partners. Welsh believes it is better to establish long-term partnerships than to gain advantage in the short term. She chuckles recalling an instance in which it seemed clear that a bank did not want to lend money, even though its ostensible business was doing just that. BOH representatives had negotiated a deal with the bank in which the rate was at prime plus one. "The problem was that prime fell so low that even at prime plus one, they weren't making anything on it," Welsh says. "We could have held them to the contract and milked them for all it was worth. But we understood that they needed to make a profit to stay in business. For the health of the long-term partnership, we proactively amended their contract in our partner's favor."

Governmental Relations: Establishing Partnerships

As Builders of Hope spreads its wings and establishes new chapters throughout America, the first entities with which it must partner are the municipalities it is entering. Five key components must be in place before organization principals make the determination to enter a new market. "Our whole basis for starting in any

Builders of Hope, doing business as EcoLogical Community Builders, is working with the city of Dallas, Texas, and the Dallas Independent School District to convert portable classroom units slated for demolition into senior cottage housing. A prototype is shown here.

new market is first and foremost establishing those partnerships," Welsh says. "We'll never go for the sake of going in just to fly a Builders of Hope flag."

The very first step for the organization is receiving *a formal invitation* from the prospective host city, setting the stage for partnership. After the initial invitation, the next requirement is for the organization to obtain *start-up funds from a local partnering agency*, such as a foundation or corporate partner. (As of this writing, the amount required to start a BOH chapter is around $300,000, translating into 18 months' worth of operating funds.) Before moving forward, Builders of Hope must determine *if a sizable inventory of homes eligible for rehab* (and in many cases relocation) *exists*. Further, BOH must identify two to three initial projects in the new area. "We don't do one-and-done," says Lew Schulman. "If we decide to partner with a city, we're committed to the long term." In the Triangle area of North Carolina, for example, Builders of Hope partnered with the Turnpike Authority, which was then in the process of tearing down 29 homes as it sought to complete Raleigh's Outer Beltline.

In addition to these primary partnerships, Builders of Hope seeks to establish an array of relationships with numerous community organizations in the new locale before making its final decision to move in. Among the groups included in this roster are the city's housing department, homebuyer assistance agencies, faith-based homeless shelters, intervention programs, and like-minded developers.

Charlotte: A Welcoming Partnership

Builders of Hope's entry into the Charlotte, North Carolina, market is a case study in the way things ought to work (but rarely do). The partnership started as most things do, with a personal contact—in this case, a lead into the deputy mayor's office. At the time, BOH management was identifying venues for which it could tap into funding provided by the Neighborhood Stabilization Program (NSP), a part of the federal stimulus package created to combat the Great Recession of 2008. Welsh realized that

Charlotte had received a sizable allocation and wondered if it had programs in place to utilize those funds. "Cities were receiving funds targeted to abandoned, vacant, and foreclosed housing, but many of them didn't have the capacity to spend the money and revitalize these blighted neighborhoods," she says.

Charlotte's leaders were extremely interested in Builders of Hope's work in areas targeted for neighborhood revitalization. "We went down and did the whole pitch to the Charlotte City Council," Welsh remembers. "Very quickly, they decided they wanted to work with us." Charlotte's interest in partnering with BOH revolved around the organization's proven ability to acquire abandoned and foreclosed properties, rebuild and sell them, and in effect transform neighborhoods that others had long ago written off.

"We want your toughest neighborhoods that need extreme rehab."

—Nancy Welsh

Nancy Welsh contrasts the Builders of Hope approach to that of other outfits in the rehab business. "Everyone is scared to death of it," she says. Reluctant rehabbers are generally looking for houses that are 10 years old and foreclosed upon—properties they can spruce up by patching holes and slapping on fresh coats of paint. "We told the city of Charlotte, 'We don't want any of those,'" she says. "'We want your toughest neighborhoods that need extreme rehab.'"

A diverse team from the city of Charlotte came to Raleigh to do due diligence and see Builders of Hope's work for themselves. Stan Wilson was the head of the Housing Department for the city of Charlotte at the time. (Wilson was so taken with the pioneering organization and its model that he has since come to work for it.) "It seemed too good to be true," he recalls. "The passion was genuine. My initial impression was that Builders of Hope covered all the key elements that you want in a partner. What's more, the organization was committed to reusing available housing stock and implementing green practices. In fact, Builders of Hope met all of the city's housing goals to expand the supply of affordable housing, to preserve the existing housing stock, and to support family self-sufficiency."

Lew Schulman puts it succinctly: "Once they saw our work, they knew it was applicable to Charlotte."

The speed with which the Queen City formed a partnership with Builders of Hope is a testament to its own entrepreneurial approach. The city's philosophy compares favorably to that of some other municipalities with which the nonprofit has engaged in preliminary discussions. Charlotteans are light-years ahead of many others, according to Schulman, because they understand how to leverage federal funding. "They don't have an issue with combining various funding streams to make projects work," he says. Other municipalities are often solely focused on working around one particular grant opportunity or source. By contrast, Charlotte approaches projects proactively, saying, "'We can pull x number of dollars from here and x dollars from here,'" according to Schulman. This approach closely mirrors that of Builders of Hope.

Like the city of Charlotte, Builders of Hope is results-oriented. "We have the ability to scale up to whatever size project the city wants us to do," Schulman says, "and we carefully document the way we spend the money, always a key component when working with government funds." This approach provides its municipal partners with a comfort zone, so they don't have to worry about HUD coming back and demanding the return of its money. "We make a point to carefully follow government guidelines, no matter how challenging or arcane," Schulman notes.

Morris Field: Partnering with Habitat

In Charlotte, Builders of Hope found a ready and willing partner—one that was as eager to roll up its sleeves and go to work as the organization itself. Not long after the Raleigh-based nonprofit offered its services to North Carolina's most populous city, Charlotte officials laid their own proposition on the table. Would Builders of Hope be interested in taking the lead on a redevelopment project that had long been on the city's planning charts?

The project they had in mind was Morris Field—city-owned vacant land in a revitalization area. Though for some time the city had been considering allowing a Habitat for Humanity community to be built on the site, leaders challenged that nonprofit to partner with another developer. They sought greater economic diversity and curb appeal, envisioning a neighborhood with escalating value—in short, staying power.

Builders of Hope principals *were* interested and quickly agreed to tackle the project. Because of its own partnership orientation, BOH management wasn't scared off by the prospect of working with another nonprofit that operated by its own rules and regulations. After all, the organization already had experience partnering with Habitat in its Fuquay-Varina community.

The invitation for Builders of Hope to collaborate in a development consisting of approximately 50 properties, of which Habitat would provide about 30 percent of the homes, represented the quintessential partnership opportunity. At the start, three players would come to the table—the city of Charlotte, Builders of Hope, and Habitat—with future funding and other partners to be identified. In effect, Morris Field would become "a mixed-income community," according to Lew Schulman. He terms this "smart planning," pointing out that disposable income is needed in every stable community.

The city of Charlotte agreed to donate land for the community at a value of around $500,000—a significant contribution but by no means a completion gift in the grand scheme of things. The overall project budget was projected to come in at around $6.5 million to $7 million, according to estimates.

Builders of Hope will employ what Schulman calls its "competencies of design" in conjunction with its partner, Habitat. For his part, Schulman welcomes having a builder-partner on the project and will bend over backward to be sure it is welcomed into the fold. "We would never want anyone to feel like the Habitat homes were for the 'poor people' in the neighborhood," he says. Historically, the city of Charlotte has provided Habitat with funding to allow for façade upgrades for an aesthetic consistency and seamless integration into overall communities. The plan is to intersperse Habitat homes in the neighborhood, making them fit architecturally. The timeline calls for work to begin in 2011. Schulman forecasts that Morris Field will become "a signature project" for Builders of Hope in Charlotte—a new jewel in the crown of the Queen City.

HUD-EPA-DOT Collaboration

From the municipal level to the state and federal levels, Builders of Hope is hard at work crafting new partnerships, alliances, and initiatives. In fact, the organization's approach to identifying areas of opportunity is demonstrated by its proactive outside-the-box thinking.

One of its major big-picture government partnership proposals was the creation at the state level of the mechanism for a HUD-EPA-DOT collaboration. Builders of Hope was instrumental, according to Welsh, in introducing legislation in North Carolina to create a task force to address how HUD, the EPA, and the DOT can partner to apply for funding and vet projects at the federal

BOH president Lew Schulman at State Street Village, the organization's first registered community meeting LEED for Homes criteria (Photo by Jennifer Kromhout)

level. BOH principals were pioneers in pulling together key players from state agencies to discuss this kind of interagency collaboration. This big-picture partnership will enable Builders of Hope (and other qualifying) projects to bundle housing, transportation, and economic development into single initiatives, rather than approaching each issue on a piecemeal basis.

"We are working with these agencies on regional smart-site planning, bringing our Green Communities model to create livable, walkable communities for the low- and moderate-income populations that have consistently been pushed into suburban or substandard urban housing," Welsh says. Through this expanding relationship, Builders of Hope has also formed partnerships with such nationally recognized leaders in sustainable urban development as Torti-Gallas & Partners and Enterprise Community Partners. This cross-disciplinary approach has far-reaching implications for whole-community revitalization that will couple single- and multi-family development with mixed-use retail, public amenities, employment centers, and existing urban landscape redevelopment. The organization's goal is for the collaborative effort to lead to a comprehensive new model for sustainable urban redevelopment.

Such collaborations cut through federal red tape in order to green-light projects and tap into allocated funds. "The issue we came across," Welsh says, "is that the money is flowing from HUD at the federal level. But DOT can't accept the money. HUD itself can't apply for the money, and there's no interagency granting or transfer at the state level." What the federal government didn't realize was that when it pushed grants to the state level, none of the partnering agencies could receive funding.

"There is a lot of stuff going on that we'd never learn about if we were just digging dirt."

—Nancy Welsh

Institutional Partnerships: On the Cutting Edge

The array of partnerships that Builders of Hope has established with universities, research institutions, and other entities is impressive and gives a window into the ambitious nature of the organization. Builders of Hope principals view these partnerships as opportunities for learning and research, for a continuous stream of fresh ideas flowing into the organization. "There is a lot of stuff going on that we'd never learn about if we were just digging dirt," says Nancy Welsh. Not only is the organization hungry for knowledge to improve its model, it seeks to be at the forefront of a paradigm shift toward recycling rather than razing outdated homes before transforming them with energy efficiencies and clever redesigns.

Builders of Hope seeks to tap into an array of human needs—from the desire to create business opportunities by being on the cutting edge of change, to the need to be generous and contribute to the greater good, to the need to educate and inspire the next generation to become innovators who refuse to accept the status quo. University partnerships also provide opportunities to give back. For example, Builders of Hope's partnership with Duke University's Pratt School of Engineering led to "Sledgehammer Saturdays"—a program that lures grad students away from their laptops on weekends to do volunteer work in the field, primarily in deconstruction prep work for house moves.

While the core construction staff at Barrington Village shouldered most of the heavy lifting, the organization benefited greatly from the efforts of numerous volunteer groups that assisted with all manner of on-site tasks. Students from North Carolina State University, for instance, landscaped a neighborhood retention pond, planting over 50 shrubs on one muddy Saturday. Wake County AmeriCorps members demolished and cleaned the debris from the interior of an entire home at Barrington Village, completing in four hours a job that would have taken the smaller BOH crew two days. Dozens of groups have similarly contributed to the work of Builders of Hope through their compassion and desire to make their communities better places.

Flexing Their Professional Muscle

Builders of Hope not only provides volunteers a chance at meaningful "grunt work" but also offers high-level on-the-job internships and training opportunities to students. In its early days, the organization worked closely with North Carolina State University's Design Center, which provided several student-intern participants. The students enjoyed hands-on opportunities to contribute to the organization's evolving design protocol. They contributed the theme and façades for Builders of Hope's premier communities, Barrington Village and State Street Village, designing elevations and incorporating such significant architectural features as welcoming front porches and a cohesive streetscape. The orientation also cleverly masked size discrepancies among homes.

Megan's Mission: "Working with what you already have"

Megan Casanega, a student in design in North Carolina State University's Master of Architecture program, worked first for Builders of Hope as an intern and later became a part-time paid employee. Casanega was identified for work at the non-profit by her advisor and mentor, NCSU architecture professor Georgia Bizios, herself a national expert in place making and residential design.

"I like working with the built environment," says Casanega, "working with what you already have. As an undergrad, I wasn't into designing for well-off people. I thought *everyone* should have design." In design school, the young student's eyes were opened to the ways in which environments were capable of changing people. Just because products were "affordable" didn't mean they should lack design. She contrasts favorably the design values of Target's product lines and merchandising to those of other big-box stores, which seem to warehouse goods with scant emphasis on design.

Casanega's work was instrumental in developing BOH's emerging design protocol—including its 3-D renderings—for the interior design elements around the green remodels. She has helped to better the lives of clients while making use of what was already there. "First, we look to see what we can salvage, then go back and draw up an original floor plan." Reflecting on her own background, Casanega says that being a small-house advocate is part of her DNA. She grew up in a small home and "never liked the transition into larger homes." Now, she is privileged to share those values with a population that is hungry for affordable design.

Social Entrepreneurship: Tapping Institutional Resources

Through its partnership with the Center for Sustainable Enterprise at the Kenan-Flagler School of Business at UNC–Chapel Hill, Builders of Hope applied to and became part of the BASE (Business Accelerator for Social Entrepreneurship) program for 2010. This selection put the nonprofit in line for guidance, mentoring, and networking and made it eligible for consulting projects for its Chapel Hill students.

Emily Egge is Builders of Hope's liaison to BASE. "The program is designed to give start-ups access to companies that have done it—companies that can provide guidance and capital." Currently, both an MBA student and an undergrad are working with BOH. One of the projects on which the graduate student is working involves exploring and developing ways to bring venture projects and investors together while quantifying businesses that factor social concern into the equation. This work, Egge says, could "revolutionize nonprofit funding sources."

Builders of Hope is also working with UNC-Chapel Hill's Master of Public Administration program, in which the professor invites class members to select projects from among those presented by businesses and community entities. The students select which projects they wish to tackle. During one recent term, students selected seven projects out of roughly 30 submissions; two of those chosen were Builders of Hope projects.

Builders of Hope principals like putting creative minds to work in helping broaden the organization's horizons and chart its destiny. One of its requests was an evaluation of the work-mentor program. To that end, students performed what Egge calls "an external audit" of the program while providing advice and direction about how it could develop, along with suggested tracking and monitoring mechanisms.

The second project selected by the UNC-Chapel Hill graduate students was "a community and context analysis" of the historic Pope Mattress Warehouse Building in Durham, which had been donated to Builders of Hope. The organization has considered many options but has never determined the best use for the facility. Should it become a work-mentor training facility? A small business incubator? Would it be better suited as storage space? Another idea floated was to transform it into a retail facility (think: Habitat ReStore) selling factory seconds or reclaimed materials from housing deconstruction to residents of neighborhoods undergoing revitalization. Nancy Welsh has envisioned such a facility where residents could buy items at minimal cost or redeem coupons for merchandise to upgrade their homes. Builders of Hope staffers are awaiting the study's recommendations.

"Dumb Homes" on Durham's Rock Street: Making Them Smarter?

An institutional partnership created by Builders of Hope and Duke University's Nicholas School of the Environment and Pratt School of Engineering holds great promise in its ongoing study of the so-called dumb houses on Rock Street in Durham. The project's official title is "Smartening Up and Sustaining Old Homes for Affordable Housing." The basic premise is this: While a privileged minority can live in high-end "smart homes," most people can afford only their preexisting "dumb homes"—that is, homes not outfitted with all the latest (and pricey) bells and whistles. Which upgrades of energy efficiency and affordability are most impactful? What are the most important upgrades average householders or landlords can make to preexisting homes to make them greener? Would an earthen roof be a wiser investment than passive solar panels? Would it be better to invest first in water-conserving plumbing or rainwater catchment?

The experiment was created in a revitalization cluster consisting of six small, virtually identical side-by-side "shotgun" houses, which will provide a kind of "test bed" for exploring and establishing new, cost-effective ways to renovate functionally obsolete homes. The goal is to use the homes as a living laboratory by retrofitting them for affordability and long-term sustainability and energy efficiency. Recently acquired by Builders of Hope in partnership with the city of Durham, the six houses occupy a property where current zoning prohibits subdivision and sale. At 650 square feet each, the houses are characteristic of low-end Southern architecture from the post–Civil War period through the 1920s. Because the homes are virtually identical—located in the same place with almost identical orientation and climatic conditions—researchers can scrutinize the effects of varying materials, elements, and variables on each one, holding one house out as a control in the experiment.

Additional project partners working alongside Builders of Hope and Duke University are the historic restoration builder Trinity Design/Build and the sustainable urban planner Civitech. In a sense, all six homes are set to become experiments in green innovation. The control model will meet BOH's current Extreme Green Rehabilitation standards. This will enable project leaders to see how its utility bills compare to prior bills for the same units.

Duke engineering and environmental students began work on two of the houses in the fall of 2010. The other four are slated to be used as student projects, with different variables. One of the unique and transformative aspects of the project is the prospect of having graduate students actually living in the homes. "Researchers would be living there, and because these homes would be rented out to grad students, there would be better monitoring, less risk of equipment damage," Egge says. This would put the students at ground zero of the experiments while providing Builders of Hope a guaranteed source of income—the kind of win-win option the organization favors.

The project has the potential to provide a significant opportunity for Duke graduate students to experience meaningful research that could generate major journal articles while making real, on-the-ground contributions to the advancement of green rehabilitation. Builders of Hope will thus become a catalyst for community engagement between Duke and the adjacent neighborhood.

Nonacademic Educational Outreach

Partnerships with educational institutions are not confined to colleges and universities. Builders of Hope staffers work with community colleges and high schools, including Turning Point Academy in Charlotte, which enrolls students in the HopeWorks work-mentor program. BOH has collaborated with Wake Tech and Central Piedmont community colleges on At-Risk Youth and work-mentor programs. And it has reached out to such nonprofits as the Triangle Chapter of the U.S. Green Building Council (USGBC), which has for two years in a row selected Builders of Hope as the nonprofit entity for its volunteer and education day.

Triangle Chapter USGBC board member Stephanie Coble describes the excitement members experienced while orchestrating a hands-on work project at BOH's State Street community for the Emerging Professionals group, which she oversees. "I was so happy to expose others in the sustainability community to the pioneering work of Builders of Hope," she says. "I was surprised to find that many had never heard of it. But once they found out about it, they were proud to take ownership in it—both for what they do and because this organization is homegrown, comes from our community, and reflects its highest shared values."

Leaders at Builders of Hope are quick to partner with other organizations and equally quick to give credit where it is due. The North Carolina Solar Center has been a key partner, one with which BOH staffers interface on a weekly, sometimes daily, basis.

Heroes Village: Housing for Veterans

Veterans represent a sizable proportion of America's current homeless population. But even veterans who are *not* homeless are often financially strapped and lack easy access to veterans' hospitals for medical and mental-health treatment.

Builders of Hope has a program called Heroes Village designed to fill this need, providing safe, affordable housing for veterans and their families in proximity to VA hospitals in Dallas and Durham. The current approach involves acquiring blighted or foreclosed multifamily buildings and transforming them with BOH's Extreme Green Rehabilitation process. On-site coordinators will be hired in both locations to provide support services such as connecting the veterans to the local communities and providing transportation. Once perfected, this program could be easily replicated nationally.

A Working Partnership: BOH and the North Carolina Solar Center

The North Carolina Solar Center (NCSC) was hired as an independent third-party verifier for portions of Builders of Hope's LEED for Homes certification, as well as a certifier and purveyor of the NC HealthyBuilt Homes Program. Its services are necessary for obtaining certification in both programs, an integral component of the BOH model.

Through working with various members of the NCSC team, but most often with Marshall Dunlap, residential green building specialist/LEED for Homes program coordinator, Builders of Hope staffers have had the benefit of learning how to implement the standards of these programs in real-life on-site situations. "Marshall has taken time and effort to not only explain the various credits but also lead discussions in how to properly construct, document, and maintain these measures," says Landon M. Lovelace, director of planning and sustainability for Builders of Hope. Lovelace credits the North Carolina Solar Center for being "an integral part of the evolution of the green building and sustainable piece" of the model.

Like all partnerships, that between BOH and the North Carolina Solar Center is a two-way street. Builders of Hope staffers work overtime to add value to the partnership. Lovelace says that

BOH's work benefits NCSC by providing feedback on "the constructability and cost" of some of the optional measures suggested for both LEED and HealthyBuilt Homes certification. "We have also worked to help simplify and make the submittal/documentation process more understandable," he says. "In our Extreme Green Rehab process, some of the measures that are straightforward in new construction have to be tweaked or adapted for rehab construction." Currently, Builders of Hope is working with NCSC to identify the issues related to better fitting some of the existing certification processes to rehab construction and attempting to resolve such issues in a collaborative manner. Similar partnerships are in place with Advanced Energy for BOH's indoor air quality and HVAC options.

The Power of One: Individual Partnerships

The primary building blocks for Builders of Hope partnerships—for any partnerships, for that matter—are individuals. It all starts with individuals, whether they be buyers or renters, employees, construction partners, bankers, or funders. Aided by the magnetic power (and sales ability) of Nancy Welsh, the high concept of the organization has drawn interest from day one. And as the organization reaches its adolescence and begins spreading its wings nationally, it continues to attract a larger and larger following.

Home donor Holton Wilkerson's partnership with Builders of Hope began one morning while he read a feature article in the *Raleigh News & Observer* about an organization that accepted teardown houses and restored them into affordable, environmentally friendly housing. He could hardly believe his eyes. Builders of Hope gave people tax credits for donating their homes—structures and materials that would otherwise be destroyed and consigned to the landfill—for recycling. "I was intrigued by the concept to the point where I went online to learn more about them and to get Nancy's contact information," he says. "I e-mailed her to see if it made sense for my house."

"It goes without saying," he continues, "that Nancy was responsive, receptive, and friendly. John [Jenkins] was phenomenal, too. Super nice." Welsh and Jenkins came to do a walk-through of the Wilkerson home, which had recently been remodeled. Granite countertops, stainless-steel appliances, and upscale cabinetry had been added to the kitchen; the master bath was tiled; and new fixtures were installed in both bathrooms. The hardwood floors were refinished, the closets improved. When Welsh and Jenkins saw the kitchen, their eyes lit up. "They immediately saw how it would translate into an amenity for the ultimate buyer."

One Gift Leads to Long-term Partnership

Donating his house to Builders of Hope was not the end of the story for Holton Wilkerson. Rather, it was the start of a fruitful long-term partnership between the private citizen and the nonprofit organization, a relationship that has taken numerous twists and turns along the way while continuing to flourish.

As broker services manager and broker in charge of Empire Properties, a preservation-minded developer and property management company in Raleigh, Wilkerson had been toying with the idea of building a new home for his growing family. He, his wife, Liz, and their toddler son had been living in a 1,300-square-foot 1955 brick rancher near the desirable Five Points section of Raleigh, a close-to-downtown community with old trees, ample sidewalks, and close-knit neighbors. Though they loved their home, their quarters were growing tight—especially as they contemplated adding a second baby to the family.

As a staunch preservationist, though, Wilkerson found himself in a bind. He didn't like the idea of tearing down a perfectly good, usable structure in order to build the larger home his family now needed. He hated to think of throwing to waste his lovingly updated home, a place to which he had added numerous upgrades since its purchase in 2002. Not only had he made the place beautiful, he was sentimentally attached to it. As the first home he had owned, it carried with it a wealth of memories—the best being his proposal to Liz in the living room back in 2003.

As the Wilkersons contemplated their expansion options, the first thing they considered was upgrading their existing home.

Holton sought the advice of several architects, all of whom argued in favor of tearing down the old house and building a new one in its place. Wilkerson wanted badly to add onto the existing structure, but the architects told him the proportions would be wrong. "It would be like turning a shoebox into a refrigerator box," he says. "You could do it, but it didn't make sense."

Since the family loved the neighborhood, teardown seemed the only option—until Builders of Hope entered the picture. Wilkerson wasn't even thinking about the financial advantages of the donation, which turned out to be considerable. The couple received a deduction for the value of the structure, spread out over five years. Wilkerson calls this "hugely beneficial." However, the biggest benefit the couple claimed was the sense of doing the right thing—for the environment, for another family, and by respecting the home that once sustained them.

The homeowner and home donor bonded instantly, her future in the home and his past converging in the present moment of celebration.

In September 2009, Builders of Hope organized a ribbon-cutting ceremony and celebration for the completion of the Wilkerson home—a flagship property for the State Street Village project. Raleigh mayor Charles Meeker was on hand, along with United States congressman David Price and numerous other dignitaries. On that occasion, Holton Wilkerson saw his old home in its final form for the first time—another remarkable image for the memory bank. "It's hard to even describe in words. As clichéd as it sounds, it was surreal to see my old house in place on Bragg Street. It almost felt like a dream," he says. "Knowing that the house was given a new life was incredibly gratifying."

At the ribbon cutting, Wilkerson met the house's new owner, Michelle Thomas, a single mother in her late 30s, and her nine-year-old son, Mason. Wilkerson told Thomas about the new baby on its way, and Thomas shared her emotions over owning a house for the first time. The homeowner and home donor bonded instantly, her future in the home and his past converging in the present moment of celebration. Wilkerson offered to bring over a house-warming gift. Thomas told him she planned to purchase a gift for his new baby. Tears of celebration fell from two faces.

Michelle Thomas: Portrait of a First-time Homeowner

On moving day, Michelle Thomas and her son, Mason, show off their beautiful state-of-the-art kitchen in the home donated by Holton and Liz Wilkerson. (Photo by Jennifer Kromhout)

Michelle Thomas was tired of pouring rent down the drain, yet it was hard to find a house she would want to own, much less one she could afford—until her mother saw a feature segment about Builders of Hope's planned State Street Village community on WRAL, Raleigh's CBS television affiliate. When Thomas looked into what BOH had to offer, she was enchanted—even more so when she found that her prospective new home was "not-so-new," a recycled beauty loaded with features she had only dreamed of, including granite countertops, solid wood floors, and even a deck on the back. It included a remarkable skyline view of downtown Raleigh. When Thomas saw that the numbers could work on her budget, she took the plunge and became the community's first buyer and resident. Probably the greatest thrill of all was seeing Mason's reaction to the bedroom of his dreams, which had been painted Carolina blue in honor of his favorite team, the Tar Heels. "Once we get a dog," says Thomas, "our dream of homeownership will be complete."

Partnership: Phase Two

After his house was moved, Holton Wilkerson found he couldn't stop thinking about Builders of Hope—the sheer improbability of this new organization appearing in front of him at precisely the moment when he needed its services. He thought of how it had been an answer to prayer. He wondered how he could stay connected and help the people he had come to admire and befriend. Wilkerson kept in touch and—after the manner of a good partner—started learning about the organization's needs. He quickly discovered that the fast-growing nonprofit was bursting at the seams. It had outgrown its offices in the planned community of Southern Village in Chapel Hill—office space that had once housed the ill-fated 2008 presidential campaign headquarters of former North Carolina senator John Edwards.

Through his work with Empire Properties, Wilkerson located a new building for the organization that would serve as its headquarters in downtown Raleigh. The building at 310 North Harrington Street had once been the offices of the David Allen Tile Company—hence the ornate tiles in gray, blue, and earth tones lining the walls of offices and bathrooms and the mirrored tiles festooning hallway ceilings. Later, the building housed Deep South Entertainment, a regional recording company, after which it had been vacant on and off for several years.

The building needed some rehab work, which the BOH construction crew was game for tackling. Wilkerson—fully supported by his colleagues at Empire Properties, who had gotten an earful about the organization—was able to secure a lease for below-market rates in exchange for BOH rehabbing the office space. "The basic building had great bones but needed reconfiguration and aesthetic updates," he says. In a booming economy, this small office building might itself have been a teardown. Directly across the street from Builders of Hope stands a symbol of the high-rolling housing market of the middle part of the first decade of the 21st century: a high-end, high-rise luxury condo building with a rooftop swimming pool and a plethora of unsold units.

Doubtless, the partnership between this inspired giver and this high-minded organization will continue to bear fruit and take new turns in the future. The wisdom of the ages says that people work together who *want* to work together. And partners like to work with partners who are looking out for each other's needs.

Captain Rob: Street Musician cum BOH Employee

Street musician Rob Frohlking came to work as a carpenter for Builders of Hope through the Raleigh Rescue Mission, a homeless shelter that helps place its residents on track for mainstreaming. Born in Charleston, South Carolina, Frohlking had drifted into homelessness after a major romantic breakup. He was also struggling with alcohol addiction.

For a number of months, the street musician—who goes by the name "Captain Rob"—played a snare drum outside the downtown courthouse in Raleigh. Frohlking fed himself with the money obtained from donations tossed into his hat. A director of contemporary worship for a Raleigh Methodist church heard him play and stopped to chat. He handed Frohlking his business card and invited him to come share his talents and open his heart to God. Frohlking took him up on the offer and began his reentry into society through the Methodist church.

When he came on board with Builders of Hope, Captain Rob drew on his background in carpentry, dusted off his Christian faith, which had been instilled in him as a boy in the Lutheran Church, and adopted a new attitude. "I try to keep doing the next right thing," he says. "It challenges my faith."

He had been on the streets for two years, living out of his backpack. He had traveled from Providence, Rhode Island, to Charleston, South Carolina, to Asheville, North Carolina. "But that gets old," says Frohlking. "I'm so grateful for this chance to turn my life around."

Stories like Frohlking's are not at all unusual for BOH's Hope-Works program. Such narratives serve to draw new partners to the organization. Doing good work with people who have been abandoned by society stands at the heart of Builders of Hope's mission to rebuild homes, revitalize communities, and transform lives.

On the original marketing materials for Builders of Hope, three key words stood smack-dab in the middle of the tagline undergirding the logo. *Partnership* sat between two other keywords—*Community* and *Opportunity*—and its importance cannot be overstated. Though that logo has since been updated, partnership remains a pillar concept for the entire operation.

One recent weekday, President Lew Schulman returned with Nancy Welsh from a fact-finding trip to a green building conference in Washington, D.C. Their goal was to scout out new partnerships, to see how they could leverage various funds to create more housing opportunities for those in need.

"We're constantly analyzing new programs to see how they fit within the scheme of development," Schulman says. For instance, the recent buzz is that federal officials recognize how difficult it is to get conventional financing for multifamily projects. Schulman set up a meeting with a regional director for Fannie Mae, the federally chartered mortgage broker giant, to discuss how the organization was handling REO (real-estate owned) foreclosed properties. Already, Schulman had a new partnership idea in mind. As Builders of Hope moves forward with a special initiative creating short-term housing for veterans, why not utilize properties that have gone through foreclosure? That would be a proactive way for BOH to help solve multiple and overlapping issues, to find appropriate housing for veterans in need while doing its part to help move foreclosed inventory through the system, all the while creating livable housing.

At the same conference, Schulman also met with program officers for the United States Department of Agriculture and learned that its programs were not limited to rural denizens. He made a promising contact with an EPA employee to try to identify funding streams there. The two agreed to meet in the coming month so Schulman could learn about new programs being rolled out and where a potential fit would be for Builders of Hope.

This proactive, pro-partnership thinking is all in a day's work at Builders of Hope. Understanding how integral partnerships are to the operation helps explain the organization's meteoric ascent, as well as its enormous promise for the future.

The Anti-greed Imperative

Being a stellar partner requires placing as great a premium on the partner's interest as on one's own. This "other-oriented" perspective offers a window into the values engendered by Builders of Hope. It also gives insight into how the organization has been able to gain traction so quickly and generate such high levels of enthusiasm from a wide swath of humanity. People are quick to warm to the model once they have been introduced. Perhaps the deepest chords it strikes are the desires to save what is already here, to reduce unnecessary waste, and to find common-sense solutions to provide humanity with its basic needs. The Builders of Hope model challenges people to find value in old houses that might otherwise fall victim to the wrecking ball. Rather than endorsing demolition and destruction—acts that are celebrated in a throwaway society—Builders of Hope calls people to salvage, rescue, and renew.

This approach hits the right note in an America that has grown weary of a national culture of greed, cynicism, and overconsumption. And people are increasingly wary of the fact that housing has become yet another disposable commodity in the national consumption landscape.

"We aren't out to make a profit," says Nancy Welsh. "Our mission is to provide affordable housing at the lowest possible cost to the greatest number of homebuyers and renters. Whatever money we can save, we pass along to our residents in the form of home equity upon closing, or reduced rents. Revenue streams go into expanding our model into new markets."

Rapid Expansion

The year 2010 ushered in rapid expansion into new markets. Builders of Hope entered New Orleans and Dallas. In New Orleans, the organization pulled off the largest documented house-rescue operation in United States history, moving a record 69 homes in 11 weeks. (Actually, it saved and moved a total of 74 homes during the operation, keeping ahead of the demolition schedule for the construction of a new VA hospital. A few of the rescue homes required special attention and extra time, due to their size and historic significance.) The homes would have been demolished without an important partnership with the city of New Orleans, led by visionary leadership and buy-in from Mayor Mitch Landrieu. Enterprise Community Partners and Providence Catholic Charities played instrumental roles in bringing this historic and history-making project to fruition.

Looking to the future, Builders of Hope managers continue to study additional markets after receiving invitations from interested potential municipal partners in Michigan, Illinois, Kansas, Georgia, and elsewhere. They continue to improve and refine the organization's pioneering model for sustainable housing while expanding its focus to assist the growing numbers of people in need of affordable rentals.

Only a Matter of Time

Despite the proven results, accolades, and winning headlines generated by Builders of Hope's pioneering work, eliminating the teardown of blighted, abandoned, and unwanted properties as the automatic first step toward revitalizing communities will continue to take work and time. But if the tipping point has not yet been reached, it will likely be in the near future. Once Americans understand that embedded in even modest housing stock are not only cultural riches but the building blocks for the nation's housing inventory, it seems inevitable that Builders of Hope's "whole-house recycling" model will take its place as the nation's premier creator of affordable housing.

INDEX

*Italicized page number indicates photograph.

ABOUT THE AUTHOR

Wanda Urbanska is producer-host of America's first nationally syndicated public TV series advocating sustainable living, *Simple Living with Wanda Urbanska* (www.simplelivingtv.net), originally on PBS stations around the country and now on hulu.com. Through her writing and public speaking, she advocates a more deeply connected, environmentally friendly way of life.

The author or coauthor of eight books, Urbanska was described by the *New York Times* as "a spokesperson for a phenomenon known as the simplicity movement." *O, The Oprah Magazine* called her "the de facto Martha Stewart of the voluntary simplicity movement," and *USA Today* dubbed her a "simplicity guru."

For many years, her mantra has been, "Nothing's too small to make a difference." Urbanska's interest in innovative, sustainable solutions led her to Builders of Hope, where she met Nancy Welsh and toured energy-efficient, right-sized rescued homes. Before long, the two women were hard at work on this book, burning the midnight oil in Raleigh and Mount Airy, North Carolina, and Warsaw, Poland.

Wanda Urbanska is a graduate of Harvard University. Her writing has appeared in *Mother Earth News*, *Natural Home*, *Glamour*, the *Washington Post*, the *Chicago Tribune*, the *Los Angeles Times*, *American Libraries*, and many other publications. She contributed to the World Watch Institute's *2010 State of the World Report: Transforming Cultures from Consumerism to Sustainability*. She is the monthly "green and simple living" blogger for the American Library Association's "@ your library website." Having lived in Boston, New York, Los Angeles, and Warsaw, she now makes her home in Raleigh, North Carolina.